sadler stories

SADLER STORIES

AND THE JAZZ BOOK

ROBERT WESLEY SADLER JR.

SADLER STORIES
AND THE JAZZ BOOK
By Robert Wesley Sadler Jr.

First Edition
Copyright © 2026 by Art Shulman

Published by
Munn Avenue Press
300 Main Street, Ste 21
Madison, NJ 07940
MunnAvenuePress.com

For permission requests, contact MunnAvenuePress.com

Paperback ISBN: 978-1-969679-37-7
Hardcover ISBN: 978-1-969679-38-4

Printed in the United States of America

In loving memory of my father,
Robert Wesley Sadler Sr.

– Contents –

– PREFACE –

MY NAME IS ROBERT WESLEY SADLER JR. I am a retired
Systems Architect who worked for the MITRE Corporation designing and analyzing system software for the Federal Government.

However, *Sadler Stories and the Jazz Book* is not about what I
did professionally. It's my memoir with an emphasis on jazz and
music, and how it kept me going. I am not a musician, but I am a
big jazz fan and a super music listener. Overall, this book chron-
icles my endeavors in education, the military, civil rights, travel,
and my professional careers, but again, with a heavy emphasis
on jazz.

I begin the book by describing my grandfather's life and how
he lived as a child during slavery in Tennessee. After the Civil
War, the saga of my grandparents and parents continued through
the American Reconstruction period. I then describe my early
childhood and teen years growing up in segregated Louisville,
KY. Civil rights and racial integration played a substantial part
in my early years. I was one of the first Black children to go to
White schools in my hometown.

The next part of the book explains how I went from Louisville to the Marine Corps and all my education, training, and work as a radar technician. I also discuss my involvement and adventures in the Cuban Blockade. But it was in the Marine Corps where my exposure and experiences with jazz began. After my military service, I stayed in California and went to college. Subsequently, I started working, got married, and had children. Afterward, I lived in Washington and Arizona, but my life with jazz continued with vigor.

I then recollect my time in Europe. Particularly, the great concerts, people, and artists that I saw and heard at the North Sea Jazz Festival in the Netherlands, the Montreux Jazz Festival in Switzerland, and the Jazz à Juan festival in France.

Music has always been with me at home, school, church, parks, and concerts. It makes me sing and dance. I especially like music that makes me think about good times, momentous events, and certain people. Jazz makes me feel the full gamut of emotions. It also incorporates many of the genres of music that I heard as a child, such as gospel, rhythm and blues (R&B), country, and classical.

I was introduced to jazz when I was nineteen years old. I first heard it on the radio in California. I was further exposed to jazz by people who were educators, musicians, and knowledge-able fans. They influenced me so much that I wanted to tell my jazz story.

- 1 -

My Parents

MY GRANDFATHER, GREEN SADLER, was born into slavery around 1848 in Dickson County, Tennessee. His father, Philip Sadler, was a White man, his slave owner, who owned several slaves, including my grandfather's mother, Cherry. All of the slaves lived in cabins on Philip Sadler's property.

Philip also had a White wife and children who lived with him in the big house. Philip's wife was very cruel to Green when he was a young child. She was particularly mean when Philip was not around. For example, she would chew bread and meat, spit it out, and order Green to eat it. She would also make Green get under the kitchen table and bark like "the dog he was." When slavery ended, Green left to start a new life.

In the 1870 Census, which is the first census that counted former slaves, Green is recorded as a twenty-two-year-old "mulatto," what we would call biracial, farm hand living in Putnam County,

Tennessee with the Ferrell family in Silver Point. Green is also recorded as being married to eighteen-year-old Martha Ferrell. They had nine children. I only know of the following seven: Lee, George, Otis, Frank, Etta, Ethel, and Matilda. Green and Martha were married for about thirty years until she became ill and passed away.

After Martha's death, Green married Lottie Jane Aiden on July 5, 1902. On their wedding night, they were given a shivaree by their family and friends. A shivaree is a marriage tradition practiced in some of the Southern states that was passed down from rural England. In this shivaree, their family made loud noises with pots and pans outside the newlyweds' house before they went to bed. The crowd then rushed inside the house, blindfolded the couple, and led them into the woods. Thankfully, everything turned out fine, as Lottie and Green made their way back home safely.

Lottie Jane was my grandmother. She was born in Dickson, TN, in 1874. She had two brothers, Osborne and Nelson. Green's marriage to Lottie Jane produced nine more children. Again, I only know of seven of them: Rose, Jessie Lee, Charles Glen, John Henry, Hubert, Robert, and Beatrice. Lottie Jane raised her children with Otis and Ethel from Green's previous marriage.

My grandmother first saw my grandfather at an all-Black barn dance. She was only twelve years old. Lottie Jane hid in some hay so no one could see her because she was underage. The barn dance band consisted of a harmonica, banjo, and drums. Green played the guitar. All the musicians sang as well. They sang the blues.

Green wore a white shirt, white trousers, and had a red bandanna tied around his neck. He was slender, light-skinned, with black curly hair. Lottie Jane thought Green was the best-looking man she had ever seen. She had no idea she would later marry him.

When they were married, Green and Lottie lived in a small house on an acre of land near Turn Bull and Colesburg, TN. These settlements are located close to Dickson, TN. Lottie Jane earned a living by washing and ironing clothes for White people.

According to Ancestry.com, Lottie Jane Aiden's parents were Lizzie Marie Sellers and Nelson Aiden, who were born around 1845 and 1837, respectively. They, too, were born into slavery. Lizzie Marie Sellers's parents were John C. Sellers, a White slave owner, and Marie Sellers, a Black slave. They were born in Tennessee about 1807 and 1824, respectively.

In the 1920 Census, Green is recorded as being sixty-eight years old and living in Dickson. He died four years later, on February 4, 1924. Afterward, Lottie Jane married Bell Henry, her second husband. Bell and my father, Robert, did not get along.

My mother's father was Tom Rivers. He was a remarkable man. He was born in June 1880 in Pulaski, Giles County, TN. His father was Franklin H. Rivers, also known as Frank Rivers, and his mother was Matilda Brown.

Tom's first wife was named Beulah. Tom and Beulah Rivers had three children: Flora, a.k.a. Courtney, born in 1903, and twin boys Wilson and Butler, who were born in 1907.

Tom Rivers married his second wife, Delia Brown, in 1914. This union produced two more children: John Thomas, born in 1914, and Anne Mae, born in 1917. Anne Mae Rivers was my mother.

The year 1917 is when Tom Rivers' life became more interesting. He enlisted in the US Army when the United States entered World War I against Germany. My grandfather was sent to fight in France. He was ranked private, and his military unit was Battery E Forty-Second Artillery in the Colored Army Corps.

When the war ended in 1919, Tom was sent home from Saint-Nazaire, France, to Newport News, VA. His ship, the Kroonland, arrived in the United States on February 18, 1919. Thomas River died mysteriously just over a month later on March 24, 1919. I do not know the cause of death, but it could have been the "Spanish Flu" or the H1N1 subtype of influenza A. The pandemic had killed thousands of soldiers returning from Europe at the time. Sadly, my mother and her brother, John, never knew their father.

My grandmother, Delia Brown, moved to Louisville, Kentucky, with her son, John, and daughter, Anne Mae, because she wanted a better education for them. My mother took advantage of this opportunity by graduating as the valedictorian of Louisville Central High School.

My father's education differed from my mother's as he only completed the ninth grade. He spent his last day of ninth grade trying to impress a girl. During lunch, Robert asked her and a couple of her friends to watch him carve the girl of interest's name into a tree. But unbeknownst to him, his teacher was standing behind him the whole time. The teacher then said, "Robert, what are you doing with that knife?" My father was expelled from school that day for bringing a weapon to school, and he never went back.

My father left Tennessee when he was about sixteen years old. His mother, Lottie Jane, sent him and his brother, Hubert, to Louisville after she discovered that they had fought with White boys. My grandmother was afraid for her sons. In those days, Black boys could be lynched or put in jail for fighting White boys. This was not their first incident of being chased or beaten by White boys, but it was the first time Robert and Hubert fought back and beat up the White boys.

Eventually, Lottie Jane sent her boys to live with their brother, Otis, and his wife, Gertrude, while my father stayed in Louisville. Uncle Hubert went to Detroit, Michigan, where he later married Aunt Helen and worked for Ford Motors. Uncle Hubert and Aunt Helen had three children: George, Margie Ann, and Jane.

My parents, Robert and Anne Mae, met at Louisville Municipal College in the 1930s. This college was for Black or "colored" students during the racial segregation period. Today, this college is a part of the University of Louisville campus. My mother attended on an academic scholarship. She majored in mathematics and minored in biology. While in college, she made money tutoring other students. She also won a prestigious certificate of achievement from Johns Hopkins University for her biology research.

Later, when I was in elementary and junior high school, I had teachers who were schoolmates of my mother. They remembered her as quiet, studious, and a brilliant student. They also said that she was genuinely nice and always willing to help.

My mother left college after her junior year. She married my father, who was a janitor there. My parents were married in 1939, which is also the year that their first child was born, Wilma Jean Sadler. My mother's family never liked my father because they believed he kept their prodigy child from achieving her dreams of graduating from college and becoming a professional.

By this time, my father was five feet and seven inches, with medium brown skin and medium weight. Robert was short in stature but considered handsome. He did not talk much, was good-natured, and had a lot of common sense. However, Robert was not athletic, and the only professional sport that he followed was baseball. His favorite team was the Brooklyn Dodgers, and his favorite players were Jackie Robinson and Roy Campanella. He followed the World Series intensely.

My father liked playing pool. In his heyday, Robert would go to the pool hall on Walnut Street once or twice a week. He was a good pool player. Robert also liked to gamble, especially when he could play eight ball or snooker. Nevertheless, he was a gambler with a conscience. He would go to the pool hall with twenty to thirty dollars in his pocket to gamble. But when the money ran out, he would quit. Sometimes, he would win, and then he would stay for three or four hours. I think the most he won was one or two hundred dollars a night.

Daddy also played golf in his early adult life. His golfing partner was Clay Thacker, who lived in Beecher Terrace about two blocks away. Mr. Thacker had two sons, Sonny Clay and Bruce. They went to school with my sister Wilma and me. Daddy had a golf bag, a complete set of golf clubs, and clothes to match. He even had the shoes. He liked golf so much that he learned the language and how to keep score. In those days, Robert could only play golf at the segregated Black golf course.

Daddy and his brothers were industrious workers. They always had jobs. If one job did not pay enough money, they would get two jobs. Sometimes, they worked around the clock. They could all cook, particularly Southern cuisine. Many times, they held cooking and janitor jobs.

Daddy also had factory and union jobs. During World War II, he worked at Henry Volts making artillery shells with his childhood friend, Ernest Evans. Later in life, he worked as a machine operator for American Builders in the steel yard. In this job, he worked with Uncle Wilson Rivers, Momma's brother. This was a union job with all the benefits. They shaped, cut, and packaged steel rods, beams, and rails for heavy construction. The end products were then used to build roads, sewage systems, bridges, airports, and high-rise buildings.

Daddy belonged to St. James Sanctified Church. He was an usher there. What I remembered most about this church was the afternoon and evening singing programs. Robert called these singing groups "quartets," although some of them were quintets or choirs. Sometimes, famous gospel singers and groups performed at St. James. The ones that I remembered were Sam Cooke and The Soul Stirrers, the Pilgrim Jubilees, the Blind Boys of Alabama, and The Staple Singers. We also listened to gospel singers like Mahalia Jackson, the Mighty Clouds of Joy, and Rev. James Cleveland on the radio. Other than church, we also heard gospel singing at the Beecher Terrace auditorium. One of Daddy's favorite singers was Kirby, a local performer.

Daddy usually worked at night, but before he went to work, he would cook dinner. When we got home from school, there would be a hot meal waiting for us. Some of the meals he cooked were roast beef, meat loaf, fried chicken, liver and onions, greens, green beans, and cabbage. He also baked cakes, pies, biscuits, and corn bread. They were all delicious.

But Daddy also had his flaws. He smoked cigarettes and loved his alcohol. He smoked one or two packs of Camels a day and drank cheap stuff like Four Roses, Thunderbird, Gallo Wine, Seagram's Seven—you get the picture. Although he drank, I never saw him drunk. Robert would drink just enough to get a buzz. He said that smoking and drinking made him feel better, so he could deal with the trials and tribulations of life.

My mother, Anne Mae Sadler, was a homemaker. She made most of our clothes when we were small. She made complete outfits, including suits, shirts, pants, dresses, blouses, whatever was needed for her family, and charged the neighbors to make some of their clothes. Anne Mae made money sewing and babysitting. This money held the household together and allowed her to buy necessities and extra things that we wanted.

Anne Mae belonged to Broadway Temple AME Zion Church and religiously took us to Sunday school and church every Sunday. When we were in elementary school, she walked us to and from school every day, about three blocks away. My mother also babysat about two or three kids, so we all marched to school in a group.

Most of my early social life was with my mother's friends and their families in Beecher Terrace.

-2-

THE BEGINNING

I WAS BORN AT LOUISVILLE GENERAL HOSPITAL in 1942. My family lived in Beecher Terrace, a housing project built for Black people. We resided in an apartment at 1022 Tenth Street in Louisville, which from the time of the Civil War to the 1960s was a segregated city. By the time arrived, Black people could still only live in certain designated areas as Jim Crow laws and culture were in full effect.

I remember growing up with hundreds of Black families with lots of children. Beecher Terrace was a self-contained community. Within the housing project were parks, tennis and basketball courts, a softball field, a swimming pool, an auditorium, a medical clinic, and an elementary school. Adjacent to Beecher Terrace on one side was Walnut Street, a major throughfare in Louisville going east–west. Along Walnut Street, there were many grocery and drug stores as well as restaurants, bars, pool halls, barber shops, and many other businesses. It was the center of the Black community.

If you wanted to go to a movie or see a concert, play, or comedy act, you went to the theaters on Walnut Street. They were named the Palace, the Grand, and the Lyric. James Brown, Sam Cooke, Ruth Brown, Dinah Washington, Louis Jordan, and many others performed at these theaters. Some of the comedy acts that performed there were Redd Fox, Moms Mabley, and "Pig Meat" Martin. Today, everything has changed. Walnut Street is now Muhammad Ali Boulevard, and most of the Black businesses are gone. Yet, other than Walnut Street, the rest of the streets surrounding Beecher Terrace were mundane and dull in comparison.

I lived in Beecher Terrace until I was about twelve or thirteen years old. My brother, Jimmy, and younger sister, Roxianne, were born when we lived there, too. My older sister, Wilma, was born in 1939, and she was about one year old when the family moved to the projects. We were one of the first families to move to Beecher Terrace, as it was an experimental project.

During the time we lived there, something very traumatic and tragic happened that forever altered our lives. My mother died. She was only thirty-three years old. One afternoon, my father came home from work and discovered my mother was ill. She was having trouble talking and eventually lost consciousness, so Daddy and a friend called an ambulance. While they waited for the paramedics to arrive, she woke up and had trouble walking. By the time she made it to the hospital, they expected her to recover and go home.

But the next day, my sister, who was nine years old then, received a telephone call from the hospital. The woman said, "Can I speak to Robert Sadler?" My sister replied, "He is at work." The woman said, "Tell him that his wife died." My sister was in shock. She told the babysitters, Aunt Ann and Mrs. Adams, what happened. They were upset and did not like the way the hospital delivered the message to a child.

My mother died during brain surgery at Louisville General Hospital on August 22, 1949. This was the same hospital where I was born just seven years earlier. She had surgery for severe migraines and blood clots. The doctors diagnosed burst blood vessels in her brain as the cause of her death. The blood clots resulted from an automobile accident that occurred during a church picnic sometime in the summer of 1948.

When my mother died, Louisville Childcare Protective Services informed my father that he would lose his children if he could not find childcare while he was at work. We would become wards of the court and be placed into foster care. Fortunately for us, this did not happen. My father had family members who were willing to take us in until he could provide childcare in his absence.

The person who took on the task of temporarily taking care of us was Aunt Beatrice or Aunt Bea. By this time, Wilma was ten, I was seven, Jimmy was six, and Roxianne was just five months old. We stayed with Aunt Bea and her husband, Uncle Mace, for about a year and a half. They lived on a 180-acre farm in Harriman, Tennessee, that was owned and operated by the Roddy family. Uncle Mace's full name was Maceo Roddy. He lived on this farm in separate houses with his mother, brother, sister, and sister-in-law. On this farm was a big red barn, a smoke house, cattle, hogs, chickens, dogs, mules, a tractor, two trucks, and various farm equipment. They also grew several crops such as corn, hay, green beans, and potatoes.

This was my first exposure to rural Tennessee and farm life. Uncle Mace built the house that we lived in, and his father and brothers built the barn. We did not have indoor plumbing, and used a well and an outhouse in its stead. Uncle Mace's father, Luke Roddy, designed many barns in East Tennessee. He was an architect by trade and college-educated.

Uncle Mace was known in East Tennessee as Reverend Roddy. He preached at two or more churches. He was a legend because he helped, consoled, and advised many people in all matters of life. But during his earlier years, Maceo Roddy worked in the coal mines in Windrock Mountain. After he received his undergraduate degree in education, he taught elementary school at Paint Rock and Emory Gap. He was later employed by the Tennessee Valley Authority at the Kingston Steam Plant. He worked there for several years as a carpenter supervisor for Russ Engineers in Oak Ridge.

Rev. Roddy was called to the ministry and served as a pastor to the Little Leaf Baptist Church in Oliver Springs for thirty-one years, and pastored the Bazeltown Baptist Church for twenty-nine. A carpenter by trade, Rev. Roddy built the two churches where he pastored. He also designed and led the building of the second Roddy family church, Oak Grove Baptist Church in Midtown, where he lived.

In Tennessee, my brother and I went to school in the basement of a Baptist church in Emory Gap. This was in a Black-segregated rural area. My teacher was Aunt Bea. There were about fifteen or twenty children in this school. The grade levels ranged from first to sixth grade. All the students were taught in one room, and we shared books.

At school, I saw a different side of Aunt Bea. She was a tough task expert and demanded a lot from her students. She expected more from me than the others because I was her nephew, and I was just in second grade. Aunt Bea led spelling bees and taught us vocabulary and arithmetic, and always used me as an example. I was always the first one she called, so I had to be prepared. I had to stand in front of the class and read passages from the textbook, spell words from the vocabulary list, and recite some of the past lessons, as well as add columns of numbers and subtract. Remember, this was just the second grade.

This was quite an adjustment for me. I came from a city school with hundreds of students and several classes in each grade, with teachers who did not demand very much from me. There were usually thirty or more students in every class, and the teachers followed a lesson plan and gave tests weekly. If you passed most of the tests, you went to the next grade, and that was that. I was never singled out to perform or to excel to excellence. When I eventually went back to Louisville public schools, I was a better student because I had mastered the fundamentals thanks to Aunt Bea. My older sister, Wilma, did not go to school with us in the Baptist church. She went to school in Rockwood, the nearest town to the farm where we stayed.

When my older sister, brother, and I returned to Louisville, we moved back to Beecher Terrace with my father. My younger sister, Roxianne, stayed in Harriman with Aunt Bea. By this time, my father had found a live-in babysitter, Miss Bertha, to watch us while he was at work. She was an older woman in her fifties and originally from the West Indies. This arrangement went on for a year until my father married my stepmother, Vivian Jones. We were lucky to have Vivian as our stepmother; she was caring and protective. We had a mother again.

Vivian also gave us another family—the Joneses—Grandma Susie, Uncle Thornton, Aunt Isabel, Aunt Grace, Aunt Dorothy, and Aunt Florence. From that day forward, we began to live as a traditional family again. Every Thanksgiving and Christmas, we would go down to Grandma's house for a big turkey and ham dinner. During the summer, Momma Vivian would take us down to Grandma's just to hang out and have fun.

My father and stepmother met in church, Broadway Temple AME Zion. Momma and her family were an integral part of Broadway Temple. Momma sang in the choir, Grandma Susie was the head of church activities, Aunt Dorothy and Uncle Theodore Dickerson were ushers, and Aunt Florence kept the church's books. Sometimes I assisted Aunt Florence in keeping the Sunday school's collection records and verifying the numbers. Broadway Temple AME Zion was my church home. It was one of the largest Black churches in town. It had many Black professionals as members, including doctors, lawyers, business owners, and office workers. The pastor was Reverend Anderson.

He later became Bishop Anderson. This church was located at Thirteenth and Broadway.

I went to Sunday school and regularly attended afternoon church services. My Sunday school teacher was Mr. Grundy. He worked as a printer downtown and had a printing shop in his house. He printed the church bulletins and Sunday school cards. Sometimes during the summer, we went to his house. There he taught and trained us how to set up the printer, apply paper, and use inks.

The head of Sunday school was Mrs. Pleasant. She was a slender, gray-haired woman in her sixties. She was an elementary school teacher who was organized and serious. Our Sunday school had classes that were separated by age and gender. My Sunday school class was for boys aged thirteen to seventeen years old. Every Sunday, we had a different lesson according to the Sunday school cards. We had special programs on Christmas and Easter, where Sunday school children performed plays and reenacted the birth and death of Jesus Christ. These plays were performed in full costumes that were designed and produced by church members. We had to practice for several weeks for these plays. Most were held on Sunday afternoons.

On a typical Sunday, we got up early, had breakfast, dressed up in our suits and ties, and Daddy drove the family to church. He later picked us up after church, and we enjoyed a big dinner that Daddy had prepared while we were in church.

Some of my friends at Broadway Temple were Virgil White, Montes Eaves, Bill Walls, and James Warfield.

- 3 -

My School Days

I ATTENDED SAMUEL COLERIDGE TAYLOR (a.k.a. S.C. Taylor)
elementary school in Louisville. It was on Thirteenth Street on
the edge of Beecher Terrace. I went to this school from kinder-
garten through the sixth grade, except for second and part of
the third grade. That was the time we lived in Tennessee with
Aunt Bea and Uncle Mace.

Some of my friends and acquaintances at S.C. Taylor were
Wendrell Watson, Mary Frances Jackson, Arthur Biller, Richard
Green, Morgan Green, Gwendolyn Hodge, Shirley Daugherty, and
Richard Bland. Unfortunately, when I moved away, I did not stay
connected with any of them. After the sixth grade, we moved to
East Madison Street. This neighborhood of Louisville was part
of the Jackson Junior High School district. In the 1950s, before
1956, Louisville had racially segregated schools. The city had
many junior high schools, but only three—DuVall, Madison, and

Jackson—were available to Black students. I went to Jackson Junior High for seventh and eighth grades.

By this time, my brother, Jimmy, and I were the only children living with my father and stepmother. My elder sister, Wilma, was married to Jack Williams, a soldier, and resided in Washington, DC. Roxianne, my youngest sister, stayed in Tennessee with Aunt Bea and Uncle Mace. Moving uptown was not the biggest news of the day. Wilma leaving home topped that by miles. We were all devastated. At first, we thought she was missing, kidnapped, or something bad had happened to her! Wilma was Daddy's oldest, and he said she was the smartest with the most potential. But Wilma also gave him the most trouble. No one knew that she was going to run off and elope. After all, she was only sixteen years old and had just passed on to the eleventh grade! It didn't help that Wilma told Daddy she was going on vacation to Detroit to visit Uncle Hubert.

We later found out that she did not go there. She went to Washington, DC, instead to marry Jack Williams. For a few weeks, Daddy did not know where she was. Jack Williams was the paper carrier who lived across the driveway in the next apartment complex. We did not know that Jack had joined the Army, as we were not friends with Jack's family and had no contact with them.

It was not until Daddy finally received a letter from Wilma explaining where she was and what she had done that we knew what had happened to her. That was a stressful time!

After we moved to the east end of Louisville, my friends were Alvin Hinkle, Sonny, and Cooley. Alvin lived next door. We played basketball in his backyard, at the recreation center, and on the playground. Although East Madison Street was not the projects, it was still a poor Black working-class neighborhood with all its associated problems. That said, moving to the east end meant that I had to re-establish myself. There were certain individuals and gangs that ruled the playgrounds, parks, and schools now and I had to stand up for myself and confront those people every day. Thankfully, after six months, things settled down and I was part of the neighborhood.

At Jackson Junior High School, the big heroes were the school's basketball players. We had several outstanding ball players: Larry Holt, Tyrone "Lefty" Henderson, Raymond Golden, Alvin Moore, and Courtney. A couple of those guys later became high school basketball stars. Raymond Golden and Alvin Moore were in my homeroom. They started on the homeroom basketball team, and I was a substitute.

After the eighth grade, Louisville integrated its public schools by law. The Supreme Court decision of Brown versus the Board of Education of Topeka, KS, in 1954 made integration the law of the land. This was the landmark case that Thurgood Marshall, a National Association for the Advancement of Colored People lawyer, presented before the Supreme Court and won. This decision reversed the previous Supreme Court decision of Plessy versus Ferguson in 1896 which legalized "separate but equal" and segregation. But Kentucky did not enforce integration until two years later, in 1956. When it finally did, this meant that some Black students would be going to White schools. Particularly, if they lived on the border between Black and

White neighborhoods. I was one of the students selected to go to integrated schools.

This was a historic event. Schools all over the South were integrating. But some cities had great resistance to integration like Little Rock, AR, Birmingham, AL. We read in the newspapers and saw on television how they were beating and harassing Black children and keeping them from attending school. After seeing all these horrible events, I had second thoughts about going to White schools. However, my parents decided that I was going to go to the nearest integrated school—Eastern Junior High on East Broadway. In the fall of 1956, my brother and I, along with about twenty-five other Black children, enrolled.

The first couple of weeks, police cars and several angry White adults lined the street toward the entry to the school.

White adults, children, and fellow students screamed, "Niggers go home!" Some of them held signs that read "Niggers go back to your own school!" or "You don't belong here!" I was fourteen years old at this point, and did not understand why White people were so angry and mean. We did not know them and had done nothing to them.

During these first weeks, I also witnessed the closest thing that I ever saw to a lynching. At the end of gym class, I heard this noise, then saw about twenty White boys in the locker room gathered in a circle yelling, "Fight! Beat him! Kill that Nigger!" They kept me outside the circle, so I could not see or interfere. They also kept me from leaving, so I could not tell anyone. In the center of this circle was the class bully on top of a small Black boy beating him to a pulp while the crowd cheered him on. The White boy outweighed the Black boy by ten pounds and was a head taller. The only thing that saved the Black kid from being beaten to death was the bell, when it rang, everyone left for their next class. I then helped the Black boy to the school office where he bled and cried. The Black boy's parents withdrew him from school that day, and I never saw him again.

About a month later, things settled down, and classroom activities were almost normal. We did not have a social life with White students or any outside of school activities. In the school cafeteria at lunch, Black students sat and ate with Black students and White students sat together. This was the most segregated period of the school day. Some of the teachers were also racist and did not believe in integration. They were not supportive or helpful. Most of them were worse than the students. They commonly referred to Black people as inferior and as having a trivial role in American history. One teacher stated in class that the main contribution of "niggers" in building America was slavery. When he said that, all the White students in class looked at me and laughed.

However, there was one exception. Harry Florence reached out to me in school. We played on the same junior high basketball team. He came to my house and took me to a nearby White Park to play basketball. This was risky because racial integration was new, and I was the first Black person to play on that basketball court. This incident went off without any problems because Harry was a top athlete and extremely popular. He was also very muscular, strong, and could take care of himself in a fight. We ate lunch at school together and talked about classes, teachers, other students, and local events. What Harry did, befriending a Black person, was unusual. Later, other White students became friendlier by taking Harry's example. His parents were working-class people and were members of the Southern Evangelist Church. According to his religion and church, he believed that all people are equal, and Black people should be treated the same as White people.

Being a Black student in a White school motivated me to become a better student. When I graduated from Eastern Junior High School, I was a straight-A student. My math teacher, Ms. Theisen, nominated me for outstanding student of the year. I was part of the graduation ceremony as the outstanding male student.

The next year I went to high school. In those days, Louisville was liberal in choosing a high school. I was interested in science and engineering, so I chose Dupont Manual, a.k.a. Manual, an engineering school. I was extremely excited to go to this school because it would prepare me to go to engineering and technical colleges. I took drafting and science courses but the drafting tools and instruments were expensive, and you could only buy them downtown at a specialty store.

I also played junior varsity football. The varsity football stars at Manual were Sherman Lewis and Paul McPherson, who were Black. Sherman Lewis ran track, and he won the state championship in the 100- and 200-yard dash. He later became an all-American half back at Michigan State University. Paul McPherson played football at Arkansas A&M. I later discovered that six-year Senate Majority Leader Mitch McConnel also went to Manual High and was in the same grade as me. I did not know him. He was not well-known in high school.

My second year of going to an integrated school was much better. Now, the dreadful thing about going to Dupont Manual was it was about five miles away so I had to ride a city bus to school. After my second year, my family moved to the west end of Louisville in a section of town named Parkland.

– 4 –

Living in the West End

WE MOVED TO A TRI-PLEX APARTMENT on Thirty-sixth and Kentucky Street, a Black middle-class residential area of Louisville where most people lived in single-family houses.

By this time, I was fifteen years old and my social life had changed for the better. Within a two-block square, there were thirty teenagers, and half of them went to Shawnee High School, the nearest and it was integrated. Across the street, I met Odell "Pooky" Ralston and his brothers Joe and Donald "Ducky" Ralston. Odell and I would remain friends throughout life. I spent a lot of time at his house just hanging out and playing basketball in his driveway.

The key to my social life then was another friend, Rudolph "Rudy" Davidson. Rudy lived about a half block away on Thirty-sixth Street. He had a twin sister, Ruth Davidson. Rudy went to Shawnee and Ruth went to Central High School, and all-Black high school. Rudy had a large network of friends. Everybody in the West End knew him. Rudy also ran track for the high school, was part of a teenage singing group, and was a great dancer. Rudy also had a girlfriend, Willa Robertson, who lived across the street from him. Willa's family owned a dry cleaner, and she went to Central High School.

Rudy had an unofficial social boys club that would meet at least once a week in the basement of his house. In this club there were Bo Cobbs, John Braxton, Michael Bibbs, Norman Miller, Rodger Henderson, Rudy, and me. The purpose of this club was to plan and have parties and other social events which we paid dues to pay for them. Rudy was president, Bo was secretary, and I was treasurer. We had great parties in Rudy's basement, especially during the summer. All the teenagers in the neighborhood between the ages of fifteen and eighteen came to our parties. We had the best music and dancers around, and the food was okay, too.

In the fall of 1958, I enrolled in Shawnee High School. This school was in a White area near Shawnee Park. I had to ride a city bus for about five miles to get there. This school was in a White working-class residential area. I was happy that I knew many Black students there, boys, and girls, as Shawnee High had fewer than 5 percent Black students and 100 percent White teachers. I took college preparation courses, particularly in math and science. My math teachers were White women, Ms. Stark, and Mrs. Sloan. They encouraged me to go further and study math. My physics teacher was Mr. Bayesian. I credit this group of teachers for their guidance and inspiration. They prepared me for later courses in math, science, and technology that I took in the military and college.

Living in the west end exposed me to middle-class values and I adopted many of their goals and aspirations. For the first time, I saw how professional Black people lived, and I had some idea how they got there. It also gave me direction. From that point forward, I knew that I wanted to be a scientist or engineer. Although this also presented a big problem, my family did not have money for me to go to college.

Despite it all, I graduated in the top 10 percent of my class. My parents were enormously proud of my accomplishments. The last month of high school was also exciting as I was going to graduate and go to the prom. For graduation, I got a cap and gown at the school and practiced for a day. The ceremony was at the school's football field. My family accompanied me to graduation. It was a great night.

But as the prom approached, I did not have a girlfriend, and I did not talk to any girl about going to the prom with me. My friend, Rudy Davidson, told me that a girl up Kentucky Street named Mattie Pearl liked me, and would be glad to go to the prom with me. So, I asked her, and she said yes. The next thing I had to do was rent a tuxedo, buy a corsage, and ask my father if I could borrow his car. He thankfully also said, yes. On the night of the prom I drove to Mattie Pearl's house and presented her with the corsage. Mattie wore a pink prom dress. She looked very pretty and grown up. Her mother took pictures of us standing together and alone. We got to prom in about thirty minutes as it was in the school gym.

There were about 300 people at prom, including fellow graduates, their dates, and adult supervisors. We danced, talked, ate, and had a lot of fun. After about three hours, some of the Black students thought it would be a clever idea if we went to Central High School, the Black school that was not integrated. Central had their prom on the same night. When we got to Central High, we saw many people that I knew. Some of the people at Central High's prom lived in the west end, some I knew from church, and others I knew from childhood. The most famous person there was Cassius Clay, who later changed his name to Muhammad Ali. We socialized for about an hour, then went home.

I graduated from high school in 1960. That summer was extremely exciting, my father wanted to take his yearly vacation in Dickson to visit his older brother, Uncle Glen, and see his birthplace. This was another first for me because it was the first road trip where I did all the driving. It was also exciting because I was going to meet Cousin Glenda. She was the same age as me and was graduating from high school, too. We had so much in common. Cousin Glenda introduced my brother Jimmy and I to her friends and showed us her high school and the town. She wanted to go to college just like me. The next fall, Glenda enrolled in Tennessee State University.

That summer, Aunt Helen and her teenage granddaughter came down from Detroit to Dickson. Aunt Helen was married to Uncle Hubert. They were on vacation, and it was the first time that I met them as well. We stayed in Dickson for a week and had a marvelous time.

I spent the rest of the summer relaxing and trying to figure out what I was going to do next. This was a tough time for me because many of my friends were leaving for college or the military. I did not want to stay in Louisville with little or no job opportunities. I really wanted to leave. So, a few days after my eighteenth birthday, I joined the Marine Corps.

– 5 –

Leaving Home

AFTER THE SUMMER OF 1960, I went to the Marines boot-camp in Paris Island, South Carolina. I took a train and then a bus to Beaufort.

Bootcamp lasted from September through December. It was a clean break from life in Kentucky. I was no longer living with or depending on my parents. My old childhood life in Louisville, KY was gone. In bootcamp, I lived in the barracks with a cross section of America: all races, people from different economic, political, and educational backgrounds. In the military, I had to fit in and become a part of a team. I was no longer an individual. My haircut and clothes looked like everybody else's. No one cared about my opinion. If I did not conform to the expected behavior of the Marine Corps, then there would be consequences.

Bootcamp was, in many ways, like gym class and football practice. You had to do pushups, run, and climb ropes. But what was different was marching on the parade field, standing at attention, running the obstacle course, shooting rifles, and learning military procedures, regulations, and Marine Corps history. Marine Corps drill instructors were our primary teachers. They harassed us every minute of the day and night that we were awake. They yelled and screamed at you. They made you run and do pushups. Everything you did was wrong. They did not call this harassment; they called it training.

When I graduated from bootcamp, I went back home for the Christmas and New Year holidays. I took a train that traveled through North Carolina, Virginia, Baltimore, and Cincinnati to finally Louisville. In Cincinnati, I had an eight-hour layover, so I visited Cousin Margie Smith and her family. They are related to the Roddy family in Tennessee. She is the daughter of Uncle Mace's sister, Roxy Roddy.

After I made it home, everything seemed different. Although I was still eighteen, most people treated me like an adult. Some of my friends had moved away, while others were still in high school, but now had different lives.

I was concerned about my next Marine Corps duty station and what I was going to do next. After the holidays, my next assignment was the Infantry Training Regiment at Camp Lejeune, North Carolina. I spent two months learning to be a basic infantry Marine. The weather was cold and damp in January. We had to live and train outdoors in the muddy fields and in tents. Sometimes the temperature got below freezing.

The Company Commander then informed me that I was going to electronic school at the Marine Corps Recruit Depot in San Diego, CA. I soon received orders to go to California, and went there by train with a group of about twenty Marines. This was a very scenic and long trip. We passed through New Orleans, Houston, and Phoenix. Finally, after three days, we arrived at the train station in Los Angeles (LA) and then San Diego.

The first thing I noticed about Southern California was the weather. I went from forty-degree winter weather in North Carolina to eighty-degree weather. Around the Marine Corps base in San Diego were roses, tulips, and petunias. I also saw things there that were not in Kentucky, like palm trees, beaches, and the Pacific Ocean. The whole place smelled like flowers and fresh ocean air.

Electronic school was like going to a military academy. Every morning, we had to exercise and go to the mess hall or breakfast before class. At school, we had military inspections, basic electronic courses, and tests. In the months that I was in electronic school, we did not have military training. Initially, there were about twenty-five students in my electronics class. After ten weeks there were eighteen Marines left. We then continued on to advance electronic courses. The ones that passed these courses would either go to radar or radio schools. I was selected to go to ground radar school for twelve weeks. I was the first Black Marine to go to radar school.

After completing ground radar school, my next assignment was Camp Pendleton, California. This was the First Marine Division. I was assigned to the First Fleet Service Regiment. My initial duty station was at Camp Pendleton, California. It was also the first place where I had a lot of time off or time for myself. This base is in San Diego County about thirty miles north of the Marine Corps Recruit Depot. My job at the base was as a radar technician in the Electronic Company, the Material, Supply, and Maintenance Battalion. I worked in an electronic shop maintaining, repairing, and calibrating radar equipment.

After about six months at Camp Pendleton, the Cuban Blockade started. This was a serious military crisis where the United States wanted to keep Russian missiles out of Cuba. I was selected to be a part of the Marine Corps expeditionary force. My military superiors did not tell us where we were going or why we were going. The only thing that I knew was we had to get about twenty vaccinations because we were going to tropical weather. Everything else was classified. We loaded all our gear, weapons, trucks, equipment, and ammo onto a flat-bottom amphibious LSD-27 ship named the USS Whetstone. This loading process took a day. We went from San Diego through the Panama Canal to the Atlantic Ocean.

The Panama Canal is an engineering wonder. It has two locks on the Pacific Ocean and two locks on the Atlantic Ocean. The canal city on the Pacific is Balboa, and the city on the Atlantic is named Colón. A lock is like a large swimming pool for ships instead of people. Ships go into this pool or at sea level, then the water level in the lock is raised to a mountain lake level. When the ships get to the lake, they usually stay there for a day or two until they can cross to the other side of the lake. Then they proceed to canal locks on the Atlantic Ocean. In these locks, ships are lowed to sea level.

After being on a ship for several months, I knew the names of 100 Marines and half the sailors. I got over being seasick in about a week but I never got used to eating sea rations and drinking powered milk. Every time we landed at a port, we got fresh fruits, vegetables, and meats. At the ports, the ship refueled, got fresh water and food.

We eventually circled the southern end of the island of Cuba for about a month, until the mission was called off. Afterward, we went to Haiti and then Jamaica. I got leave for a day in Haiti. It was a Black country where they spoke French. The people were friendly and anxious to sell you their goods, food, and clothes. Next, we went to Puerto Rico to a fort named Roosevelt Roads. Afterward, we went to a Puerto Rican island named Isabella Segunda that the US Navy uses for rest, fuel, supplies, and target practice. Then we went back through the Panama Canal to San Diego and Camp Pendleton.

– 6 –

No Remnants of the South

BEING AT CAMP PENDLETON in California in 1962 gave me a sense of freedom. For the first time, I felt like I was out of the South and away from Jim Crow. Politically, socially, and economically, this place was quite different from the South. I did not see any signs stating, "Whites Only" or "Colored," and there were no statues of Confederate soldiers in public facilities. Restaurants, waiting rooms, and hotels were racially integrated. I felt like I could go to any place, public or private, just like anyone else, without any negative consequences.

Some White people even greeted me by saying "Good morning" or "Have a nice day" with that carefree California attitude. It was quite refreshing. I appreciated California's easygoing lifestyle. California in the 1960s was brand new for me. I could go to restaurants, hotels, and beaches without getting locked up or chastised. For the first time, I went to Chinese, Mexican, and

Italian restaurants, and found the food different and delicious. These things were not available to me, or were illegal, in the South in the 1950s and 1960s.

California in the 1960s offered free junior college education and plentiful jobs. It seems like everyone had something to do, was working, and was going somewhere.

Some of the industries that were booming at that time were electronics, aerospace, automotive, entertainment, and housing. California was the place to be. The want ads in the local Sunday newspaper were an inch thick.

I decided that this was the place that I wanted to live.

Young people, ages eighteen to thirty, were migrating to Southern California from all over America. It was a perfect place to meet people, go to school, and work with people with the same interests, particularly young Black people from the South who had dreams or opportunities denied or suppressed because of Jim Crow laws.

What made this period extra special for me was reconnecting with my childhood friend, Odell "Pooky" Ralston. I have known him since high school and we are the same age. Odell lived across the street from me in Louisville. We went to the same school, Shawnee High School. Sometimes he drove me to school in his old used Ford. In the eleventh grade, we were in the same homeroom. Odell was also a high school basketball star. He started on the team and was in the newspaper multiple times as the outstanding player of the game.

In the last two years of my Marine Corps service, I went to LA on the weekends to stay with Odell. He lived in South

Central LA, a little off Broadway, in a house with two brothers from Beaumont, Texas. The brothers were John and James Taylor. They went to high school with Odell's first wife. They had introduced them. Odell and the Texas brothers worked at General Motors in Long Beach. They met many people at work, which resulted in them having friends of all races all over town.

South Central LA was full of Black people in the 1960s from Texas, Louisiana, Mississippi, and other Southern states. There were plenty of Black churches, night clubs, and beer joints in this section of town. This part of LA looked like a part of the old South and was adjacent to Watts and Compton. Most of the young Black people that I met here were interested in R&B. They liked R&B music from Motown, Philly, Chicago, Memphis, LA, and New York (NYC). This was the music that they listened to on the radio and at parties and dance clubs.

However, South Central LA was a blues and gospel town in those days as well. Most older people from the South that I met talked about B.B. King, Bobby "Blue" Bland, Muddy Waters, John Lee Hooker, just to name a few. There were also a few local blues singers like Johnny "Guitar" Watson and Etta James who were extremely popular. But I cannot forget about the church people. They talked about their preachers and choirs as though they were celebrities and the best performers in the world. Local gospel radio stations featured Reverend James Cleveland, Mahalia Jackson, Andraé Crouch, Walter Hawkins, and others. It was hard to find anyone who was interested in jazz or other music genres.

My first experience with local music in LA was blues at Brass Rail. This place was the type of gut-bucket club that you can find in almost any Southern town. These night clubs are on the Chitlin' Circuit. The entertainment was superb. Some examples of the great performers were comedy duo Skillet and Bucket, Big Mama "Hound Dog" Thornton, Moms Mabley, and others. It was not jazz, but it was incredibly good down-home blues and comedy.

– 7 –

LAST MARINE SCHOOL

IN MY LAST TWO YEARS in the Marine Corps, I was selected to go to Radiation Monitoring Equipment School. This was a Navy school at Treasure Island Naval Base located in the bay between San Francisco and Oakland. Radiation monitoring is part of the military's Nuclear, Biology, and Chemical (NBC) programs. The Navy has one of the NBC elite programs because of its nuclear submarines and aircraft carriers. Nuclear reactors on these ships can leak and cause a disaster, so keeping radiation under control is paramount.

The Radiation Monitoring School lasted two weeks, every workday, and eight hours a day. The course covered photo multiplier tubes, Geiger-Müller counters, film badges, and other radiation detection devices. A major part of the course was using, maintaining, and calibrating equipment. Safety is a key feature of radiation monitoring. Humans can only be exposed to a certain amount of radiation before becoming critically ill or dying. Calibration and measuring detection devices are done by using a radiation source like Cobalt-60. All radiation sources must be locked up in a control environment. As a result, classroom and laboratory work in this school required me to be alert, careful, and cautious with dangerous materials. I was glad when that course was over, and I passed it.

However, the Radiation Monitoring School was not all study and books. I also had fun and saw people who I had not seen in years and toured and shopped in San Francisco.

During lunch one day, I ran into a female sailor who I had not seen since elementary school. Mary Frances Jackson was serving meals on the chow or buffet line. The last I heard of her she was a cheer leader for Central High School back in Louisville. When I was going down the chow line, she screamed out my name, "Bobby Sadler!" I was surprised because nobody had called me that for several years, especially in the military. It was good to see and talk to a hometown girl out in California.

In the evenings after class, I went to the base gym to exercise and play basketball. There, I encountered another acquaintance from my hometown, Albert Capers. He lived down the street from me back home. We talked and played ball. He was serving in the Navy as a reservist.

On the weekends, I left the base and toured San Francisco where I went downtown to look at expensive clothes in department stores and ate at some fancy restaurants. I wanted to see famous city sites, so I took a bus tour so I could see Fisherman's Wharf, the Golden Gate Bridge, Sausalito, Union Square, and Chinatown.

– 8 –

First Jazz Encounter

IN 1962, I WAS AN E-3 or lance corporal in the Marine Corps and just getting back from a deployment in the Cuban Blockade. I was stationed at Camp Pendleton, about fifty miles north of San Diego and about 100 miles south of LA. It was a convenient location because it was close to many music, cultural, and political events. There are also about five major universities within a 150-mile radius that have several jazz concerts during the year.

In those days, I talked about jazz and music, or anything else in general, with my friend and fellow Marine, Major Thrower. Major is his first name and not his rank. He was from NYC, attended private schools, studied music and the classics, and played guitar. Major went to all types of concerts all over the city with his family and friends as a teenager. He heard jazz, particularly, in the Village and Harlem. Although he liked jazz, his favorite guitar player was the Spanish classical guitar player

Pablo Casal, and his favorite piano player was Horowitz, the classical pianist.

Major went to some of the great jazz clubs in NYC, such as the Village Gate, the Palladium Ballroom, the Village Vanguard, Five Spots, Minton's Playhouse, and Birdland. I wondered how he did all those things as a teenager. When did he have time for school? How did he get into places when he was not twenty-one? Somehow, Major managed to get in those places and saw jazz greats like Miles Davis, Dizzy Gillespie, Charlie Parker, Duke Ellington, Art Blakey, Sonny Rollins, and Thelonius Monk. This was the bebop era of jazz. Major thrived in that environment and met many jazz musicians and fans. His experience differed significantly from mine. I heard jazz for the first time on the radio one night in California when I was nineteen years old. I did not know much about it, but I liked the music. I considered Major to be a jazz expert.

Major and I got along well because we were both nineteen, E-3, and the only Black Marines in the company. This company was an electronics company in the Material Supply and Maintenance Battalion. We were both also interested in Black history, education, and music, of course.

But Major and the other Marines from NYC thought the world began and ended with NYC. Being with them was like taking a cultural and geological tour of NYC. They talked about all the sites and places of interest there, such as Central Park, the Empire State Building, the Statue of Liberty, Rockefeller Center, the United Nations, the Metropolitan Opera, Madison Square Garden, the Guggenheim Museum, etc. They also bragged about the subway system and how easy it was to travel around NYC, and all the weird people that you saw. They used the subway to go to Brooklyn, Queens, Yonkers, and Harlem in a few hours.

In the Marine Corps, Major and I spent a lot of time together. Everybody called each other by their last name there, so he was Thrower and I was Sadler. We made a natural pair. He was from the North, and I was from the South. He was from NYC, and I was from the country. He went to private Catholic schools, and I went to public schools. What a contrast in backgrounds. Needless to say, these differences gave us many things to talk about.

Before meeting Thrower, the type of music that I was familiar with was R&B, gospel, and country. All the stuff that you hear on the radio in Kentucky. One day, Thrower said that we were in luck. One of the great jazz players from the Miles Davis Quintet was coming to town with his own group, "Cannonball" Adderley. This would be a wonderful time to catch some live jazz music, and this opportunity was rare because great jazz musicians never come to San Diego. I was excited!

The concert was at the San Diego Grand Hotel in the middle of town, and to my surprise, it was sold out. We were lucky again because we got tickets just in time. Thrower reminded me that going to jazz concerts was important so we should dress up in our Sunday best. However, I did not have that kind of clothes, so I went downtown and got an expensive charcoal gray suit with a tie, shirt, and shoes to match. I also got some cologne, so I would smell good. Now I was ready to go. On the night of the concert, all the Marines in our barracks thought that we were going to a wedding, and that one of us was getting married. We quickly dispelled that rumor as those kinds of stories spread like wildfire.

Surprisingly, my new suit took on a life of its own. Everybody in the Electronic Company knew about it. Within six months, a couple of Marines wanted to borrow it for family or special events that they were attending. But Thrower was right about the concert being a dress affair. All the men wore suits, and the ladies wore church-like dresses. Cannonball and his band wore dark blue suits. Later, I discovered that this band consisted of some famous musicians: Cannonball's brother Nat Adderley, Sam Jones, Bobby Timmons, and Louis Hayes. They played one of their best songs called "Dis Here" that I really liked. This concert did not disappoint; it was outstanding. Every song was entertaining, and Cannonball explained each one. That was my initial jazz concert.

During the months that followed the concert, I went downtown to Oceanside and San Diego to record stores and the Navy Exchange. I browsed through all the jazz albums and music that I could find by Cannonball, Miles Davis, Coltrane, Charlie Parker, and Dizzy Gillespie. I learned so much from reading the album covers and the contents. Sometimes I would listen to their music at the record stores for hours. I was hooked on jazz. I picked up a copy of Miles Davis's *Kind of Blue* record and played it so much that some of the guys started to call me Miles. What I liked about this album was that it was easy listening and smooth. It featured Miles Davis on trumpet, "Cannonball" Adderley on alto saxophone, John Coltrane on tenor saxophone, Wynton Kelly on piano, Bill Evans on piano, Paul Chambers on bass, and James Cobb on drums. My favorite piece on this record is "All Blues," because all three horn players played great blues solos. I also liked two other songs on the album, "Freddie Freeloader" and "So What," because they are twelve-measure blues and sixteen-measure of one scale, respectively. In other words, it is blues played in a jazz format and played by jazz musicians. Miles clearly broke away from bebop and the influence of Charlie Parker on this album. *Kind of Blue* has a slower and smoother sound than the hard-driving and fast rhythms of bebop. This kind of music is called smooth jazz.

After going to the record stores and listening more intensely to the jazz radio stations, I began to appreciate other jazz artists out of the NYC bebop era like Horace Silver, Art Blakey, Max Roach, Clifford Brown, Sonny Rollins, Kenny Dorham, and more.

– 9 –

SECOND JAZZ CONCERT

THE SECOND JAZZ CONCERT came out of nowhere. It occurred when I was in the Marine Corps as well. We were all sitting around in the barracks, and Sonny Arias said, "How would you guys like to go up to LA to hear my father play?" My initial answer was no. I did not want to spend my weekend and money with a bunch of Marines bumming around LA. I spent enough time with them at the base. But some of the other guys thought it was a great idea.

I also had no idea who his father was, who he was playing with, or where he was playing. All I knew about Sonny was that he was from Chicago, and we spent time together playing basketball and touch football, and going to the Enlisted Men's Club. Sonny was in a Supply Company along with other friends like Harry Brown, R.L. Brown, Zeke, and Larry. I liked hanging out with them as we had a lot of fun. One of my best friends in this group was Harry Brown from Denver. He was about 6 feet and 1 inch and all muscle. He was also very athletic, talkative, and easygoing. We mostly talked about sports.

I was very surprised to learn that Sonny's father was Eugene Wright, the famous bass player with the Dave Brubeck Quartet. He also told me that next month, Dave Brubeck and his band were playing at Shelly's Manhole in Hollywood, one of the premier jazz spots on the West Coast. Sonny Arias said if we were interested, his father could get us into the concert for free, and we could meet the band.

I was excited because Dave Brubeck had Paul Desmond on saxophone, whom I listened to on the radio. He was one of my favorite musicians. He had a soft and smooth sound. In the 1960s, some of the other big names of West Coast jazz were Stan Kenton, Gerald Wilson, Wes Montgomery, Cal Tjader, Frank Morgan, Mose Allison, and The Jazz Crusaders. West Coast jazz musicians were not as hardcore bebop, eccentric, and well-known as the East Coast jazz musicians.

On the Saturday of the concert, we met Eugene Wright at the famous Brown Derby Restaurant in Hollywood for lunch. This place was a well-known hangout for movie stars and the who's who of LA. We were all looking around to see if we could recognize anyone famous. But we had no such luck. We did not see anybody who looked remotely famous or rich. I then focused on the menu and selected a cheeseburger. It was incredibly good, much better than the burgers back on the base. Before we left LA, we saw the Hollywood Bowl and the famous Hollywood sign.

The concert was great. Dave Brubeck played two of his big hits: "Take Five" and "Blue Rondo à La Turk." Afterward, we connected with Eugene Wright again, and he was nice and talkative. He told us that Sonny played the drums and asked him about his plans after he left the Marine Corps. He wanted him to return to Chicago and continue playing the drums and studying music.

I enjoyed Dave Brubeck's music immensely. It was different from the NYC jazz that I heard on the radio. It was a blend of smooth jazz and classical. After looking into Dave Brubeck's background, it all made sense. Brubeck was raised on a ranch in Concord, California. He got a four-year degree in music before he was drafted into the Army during World War II. Brubeck played in the Army band, and then studied music in graduate school, specializing in music structures and orchestration. You can hear the influence of his educational background on his music.

When we got back to Camp Pendleton, I could not wait to query Sonny Arias about his musical training and background. He admitted that he had studied music since junior high school, particularly piano and drums. In high school, he was a part of the marching band, and he took private music lessons. Since he liked the drums, his father, Eugene Wright, brought him a set of drums and albums by great jazz drummers such as Art Blakey, Max Roach, and Gene Krupa. His father told him to copy the music that he heard on the albums and to practice the drum solos.

Overall, his father wanted Sonny to be exposed to jazz orchestration so he would see how he could fit into that type of music structure. He brought him albums by Duke Ellington and

Count Basie. They listened to these albums together, and his father pointed out the important places that change the rhythm of the song.

Sonny was from a musical family. His mother and sisters were singers, and they had an even bigger influence on him than his father. They sang in the church choir, and his mother played the piano for the church as well. Chicago is a blues town. Sonny's mother and her friends knew a lot more about blues and gospel than jazz, so most of the music that was played in his house was blues and R&B. They also knew and frequented the famous night clubs and dance halls on the south side of Chicago where Muddy Waters, Howlin' Wolf, and Little Walter played. His parents heard the live performances of Dinah Washington, Fats Waller, and Lionel Hampton. They also knew the great churches where Sam Cooke and The Staple Singers performed. Sonny had a rich musical background.

Back in the barracks, we spent many nights sitting around listening to R&B albums. My favorite R&B musicians at the time were Smokey Robinson, Luther Vandross, Jerry Butler, James Brown, Sam Cooke, and Little Anthony. R&B was played a lot because it was good dance music, and it reminded the guys of back home.

– 10 –

JAZZ IN COLLEGE

I LEFT THE MARINE CORPS in 1964. After four years in the military, I wanted to do something entirely different and follow my original plan of going to college. This was a dream come true, and UCLA was an excellent choice for me. It was in California, with great weather, and near the beaches. Also, it was a top-rated university. I did not have to travel far from Camp Pendleton, and I could live in the dormitory where I did not have to cook meals. I also had instant friends and housekeeper services. I resided on the fifth floor of Sproul Hall. I was happy to be back in the classroom again.

Although these were not my first college courses, it was the first time that I lived on a college campus and went to classes outside the Marine Corps. UCLA in those days had a large White and upper-middle-class student population from Southern California. The atmosphere and culture were different from Louisville.

I took several courses, including mathematics, political science, and engineering. But the ones that really stood out were the jazz courses. I majored in mathematics and minored in computer science. Jazz was in the liberal arts and considered an elective. I wanted to do something entirely different and fun, because my days in the Marine Corps were so structured and routine. The jazz courses that I took were "Introduction to Jazz" and "Jazz Structures." Dr. Tanner taught them. He was a professional musician who played for recording studios and movie companies. He also played with Stan Kenton and Shelly Manne.

Aside from music, I had a famous Black political science professor. His name was Dr. Charles Hamilton and he coauthored *Black Power* with civil rights activist and organizer Stokely Carmichael. Dr. Hamilton was a distinctive and stylish individual. He wore flashy sport jackets, white shirts, and bow ties. He reminded me of a Black Southern Baptist preacher because of the way he talked and delivered his lectures. But I was itching to talk to him about civil rights and why he did not talk about it in class. So, one day I scheduled an office hour session with him to find out how he felt about the civil rights movement, Martin Luther King, Malcolm X, and the Student Nonviolent Coordinating Committee. After this meeting, my opinion of Dr. Hamilton changed. He was not the person I thought he was.

Dr. Hamilton was glad to see me and grateful that I was interested in civil rights and voting legislation. But I found out he was heavily involved in the civil rights movement in Chicago, and that he was a presidential adviser on race relations to President Kennedy. He said that he talked to the president's brother Bobby many times about the status of Black people in the United States and what could be done to help their situation. Before I left his office, he said young Black students like myself were popping up all over the country and changing the status quo, and protesting for civil rights. He then thanked me for being a concerned and active participant. I was awestruck.

Back to jazz. The jazz courses at UCLA discussed the elements of jazz, like having a pentatonic scale instead of octaves, blue or C notes, call-and-response, falsetto breaks, blues themes and improvisations, African rhythms, and instruments. These elements differentiate jazz from European classical music. Jazz has its roots in blues, gospel, and classical music. Organized jazz started in New Orleans and branched out to Chicago, NYC, Kansas City, and the rest of the United States. Eventually, it became a world music genre.

Dr. Tanner often stated that jazz and music are performing arts or listening arts, and that the best way to learn about jazz is to listen to it and try to understand what the musician is trying to convey. Some of the various jazz musicians he played for us in class were Sidney Bechet, Louis Armstrong, Benny Goodman, Duke Ellington, Count Basie, Glenn Miller, Stan Kenton, Louis Jordan, Billie Holiday, and Charlie Parker. More importantly, he played a Mahalia Jackson gospel song, "In the Upper Room," that had a full range of voices: tenors, sopranos, altos, and basses. He demonstrated how the voices could be imitated by jazz instruments like the saxophone, bass, drums, guitar, and trumpet. Jazz uses a lot of elements of gospel. He played a blues song by Ray Charles, "I've Got a Woman," and pointed out how blues influenced jazz. This song has a classic twelve-bar blues theme and improvisation, like many jazz pieces. For example, "I've got a woman way over town that is good to me" is exactly twelve words (i.e., bars or measures). This phase is called the theme in jazz; it is repeated twice, then the musicians play the improvisation. In the last part of the song, they play the theme again.

One of the textbooks that we used for the jazz classes was by LeRoi Jones, now known as Amiri Baraka. The book, *Blues People*, was a history of African music, especially West African music, and how American blues and jazz were influenced by it. Baraka was a Black civil rights activist, writer, and poet from New Jersey who frequented many jazz clubs in NYC during the '50s and '60s.

The jazz courses also discussed some of the important places where jazz developed in the United States, such as New Orleans, and how each place had its unique style and musical sound. Other major hubs of jazz were Kansas City, Chicago, LA, Philadelphia, Washington, DC, and NYC, of course.

The jazz courses at UCLA gave me a foundation in jazz and a better appreciation of music in general. From that time forward, I tried to identify the elements and structures of jazz whenever I heard records or concerts. Sometimes avant-garde or experimental jazz does not follow traditional jazz patterns, and it is difficult to identify its elements.

- 11 -

More California Jazz

I moved to Santa Monica, California, in the fall of 1964 because UCLA was too large and expensive. I transferred to Santa Monica City College (SMCC). This junior college was ideal because it was inexpensive, near the beach, and I did not have to move far. But going to this college was like starting over again.

I had to find a place to live, enroll in school, and find a job. I found an apartment that was advertised on the college bulletin board. It was on Nineteenth Street, about two blocks from SMCC. My roommates were former college athletes. The most well-known was Warnell "Dip" Jones. He was about 6 feet 10 inches from Centerville, TX, and played center for UCLA's basketball team in the early 1960s. The other two roomies were from Philadelphia and played basketball and football for Antelope Valley Junior College in Lompoc before moving to Santa Monica. None of these guys attended SMCC. The Philadelphia guys had hopes of getting athletic scholarships to four-year universities, then playing professional ball. Unfortunately, the latter would present a problem. They ended up having too much free time, which interfered with my studies. Sadly, their dreams and aspirations of becoming professional ball players never materialized.

The guy that I had the best relationship with was John "Poppy" Pemberton. The other roommate was Mike Jordan, not the famous Chicago Bulls basketball player. The Philadelphia guys went to Overbrook High School and played high school basketball. But they knew famous Philadelphia basketball players who were professional ball players, such as Wilt Chamberlain, Wali Jones, and Walt Hazzard. Sometimes when these ball players came to town, they would visit them and go to their ball games.

I found a job at UCLA Hospital as a medical records clerk. This job was ideal because I could work at night and go to school during the day. I also kept my connection to UCLA by going to the student union, the bookstore, and the library whenever I had time.

I wanted to broaden my knowledge of music, so I enrolled in a couple of European classical music courses—"Introduction to Classical Music" and "Music Appreciation." I also took calculus and physical anthropology.

But the first semester at SMCC changed everything for me. That's because I met the love of my life. One day in the school cafeteria, a female friend of mine, Jeanie Johnson, introduced me to this tall, beautiful, Black girl named Carole Brown. This first meeting was a non-starter. We both said, "Hello, it is nice to meet you," and then went on to our classes. However, after several weeks, my roommates and a couple of guys from UCLA decided to go to the SMCC gym to play basketball. I thought this was a promising idea, so I went along with them. When we arrived on campus, the guys headed straight for the cafeteria to get something to drink. Carole Brown was sitting at a table alone. One of the guys with us, a UCLA linebacker, headed right toward her. He said, "I am going to talk to that girl." The place where she was sitting was the only empty table available, so we all sat there. The linebacker immediately started to whisper into Carole's ear. After about two minutes, she stood up and told him that she had to go to class. Then she looked at me and asked, "Will you walk me to my class?" Everyone at the table was surprised, especially me and the linebacker.

I immediately jumped up and said, "Sure, I would be glad to." I could see that she was a little uneasy and embarrassed by the situation. I tried to lighten up the conversation by saying, "What is the matter, you did not like that guy"? She laughed and said, "He was ugly, pushy, and had bad breath." We then laughed all the way to her class. When we got to the threshold of the classroom, Carole told me that she really enjoyed our conversation and wished that she did not have to go to class. Then she went through the classroom door.

We met again the next day and made a date for the movies on the weekend. The movie was great, but I do not remember it. It was probably a James Bond movie or Zorba the Greek. But I remembered that we had an enjoyable time. The following weekend, I had a music class assignment to review a classical concert in downtown Santa Monica at the Civic Center. Since I had just met Carole, I wanted her to go with me, but I did not know how she felt about going on this kind of date. I asked her and I was pleasantly surprised. She and her mother had been listening to classical music for years, and she said that she would love to go. The classical concert was Tchaikovsky's *1812 Overture*. Carole enjoyed the concert, and I wrote my review and turned in the assignment.

The next few weekends, Carole and I went to a couple of movies, museums, and restaurants. Then it was time to do another classical music assignment. This time, I had to attend an opera and review it. I chose *Madam Butterfly* because it was currently performing and local. Carole went to the opera with me, and we both enjoyed it.

Later, I discovered that Carole was taking a modern dance class that emphasized jazz, and she needed some jazz music for her final dance piece. After listening to several albums, she decided on Miles Davis's "Sketches of Spain." Her teacher liked her music selection, and they choreographed a dance skit around it. She got an A in that class.

Santa Monica and West LA did not have a lot of live jazz at the time, so I listened to the radio, where we heard new jazz singers like Roberta Flack and Nancy Wilson. Carole liked them so much that we went downtown and bought their albums. I also bought a few R&B records for myself by The Temptations, Smokey Robinson and the Miracles, The Four Tops, and Marvin Gaye. My roommates and friends played this music at their house parties for the next few months.

Thankfully, the surrounding areas were loaded with live jazz venues. Hollywood and LA had plenty of venues and clubs to hear jazz, and just south of Santa Monica at Hermosa Beach was The Lighthouse Café, a famous jazz club. This place had some great jazz, and famous musicians played there weekly. Carole and I went to many jazz concerts in Hermosa Beach. We heard there were a couple of outstanding concerts by Jimmy Witherspoon, Willie Bobo, and Mongo Santamaría.

Jimmy Witherspoon wore a red leather bolero jacket and blue jeans. He was about 6 feet 4 inches tall, and an imposing figure. Every time he sang, "God Bless the Child," he had a shot glass in one hand and would occasionally take a sip.

Mongo Santamaría was a fantastic bongo player. He sat with his legs around bongo drums, raising his hands to their fullest extent. He was extremely fast and rhythmic. He said that he played bongos in the Cuban style. I had never seen anyone play like that before. The other artist on the program was Willie Bobo. Previously, they played together in Cal Tjader's band.

In 1966, I moved to LA for a couple of weeks. There, I moved to a rooming house owned by a young Black guy, Art McBride, who worked as a security guard for General Motors in Long Beach. Art was an Air Force veteran. I moved to this house because my homeboys, George Glass and Victor Trice, lived there. They were old friends who went to Sunday school with me back in Louisville. They had just gotten out of the Navy and were trying to establish themselves in California. George and Victor were best friends. They lived together and worked at the same bank.

George was tall, good-looking, and had wavy hair. He also had excellent communication skills and worked as a loan manager at the bank. His aunt was a famous jazz singer, Helen Humes. She introduced George to Natalie Cole, The Mills Brothers, and other Black celebrities. George had a lot of lady friends. His main girlfriend, Marilyn Caldwell, was from New Orleans and worked downtown in the financial district.

Victor was average-looking and did not have George's outgoing personality. He worked at the bank as a clerk. All of Victor's friends tried to find him a girlfriend, but we were unsuccessful.

After a few weeks of living in LA, I missed Carole, so I moved back to Santa Monica. As soon as I did, we began to go to more music and dance events, especially house parties and concerts. There was a jazz club named Memory Lane. This club had wonderful Sunday afternoon matinees. There we saw Gerald Wilson's band and The Young Rascals. These were Carole's favorites.

Carole and I were married in 1966 and had two children, Hilary, born in 1967, and Robert, born in 1969. We lived in Santa Monica and LA from 1966 to 1970. During this time, I worked several jobs as an electronic technician and computer programmer for companies such as Hughes Aircraft, Korad, and the Litton Industries.

— 12 —

UCSD, Ralph Smith, and African Jazz

IN 1970, WE MOVED TO CLAIRMONT, a section of San Diego County. Initially, I worked for a job training program at the University of California at San Diego (UCSD) to teach computer programming skills to disadvantaged young adults, mostly Black and Brown poor people, in the San Diego area. I worked as an instructor for a project named Computer Jobs Through Training (CJTT). This program was started and headed by Dr. Granger Morgan, a former PhD student at UCSD. He later went to Carnegie Mellon University and became a professor and department head of the environmental engineering department.

While teaching for CJTT, I met fellow teachers Brad Rogers, Curtis Bagley, Delvin Williams, Mike Mesa, and Norm Downs. Except for Norm Downs, all the other teachers were part-time, minority, and full-time students at UCSD's Third College. This was an experimental college headed by Dr. Joe Watson and created to aid underserved college students in their pursuit of higher learning. The Third College was unique because all of the required general education courses were in Black or Latinx history, culture, and liberal arts.

Brad Rogers was the student instructor with whom I spent the most time talking about music and computer science. I called Brad my blues man, because he knew everything about blues and had this vast collection of blues records by B.B. King, Muddy Waters, T-Bone Walker, John Lee Hooker, Albert King, Big Joe Tuner, Buddy Guy, Junior Wells, Bobby "Blue" Bland, Lightin' Hopkins, Howlin' Wolf, Sonny Boy Williamson, and others. We spent a lot of time listening to Brad's record collection.

Brad's favorite instrument was the guitar and he liked acoustic and electric guitars the most. He thought the best guitarists were B.B. King, T-Bone Walker, and Jimi Hendrix. Brad pointed out how the blues influenced jazz. Brad was from Texas and loved the blues people from Texas. Some of his favorite Texas-born blues players, were Eddie "Cleanhead" Vinson, T-Bone Walker, and Lightin' Hopkins.

While working as an instructor at CJTT, I continued going to college. In 1972, I graduated from San Diego State University with a BA degree in mathematics and a minor in computer science. My family and coworkers attended my graduation at the San Diego State football stadium. We had a big party afterward on a houseboat restaurant in the San Diego Bay.

After the CJTT program ended, I worked as a scientific programmer for Gulf General Atomic, a company that designed and produced nuclear reactors. In this job, I wrote programs from mathematical equations and scientific methods for nuclear reactors in the Fortran programming language. This company was in Torrey Pines. Brad Rogers also worked at General Atomic as a systems programmer. We continued listening to my jazz and his blues music.

In 1976, my family and I moved again. This time to Solana Beach in the northern part of San Diego County. I worked for a company named TRW as a systems programmer. By this time, I had developed quite a collection of musical albums consisting of jazz and R&B from the '50s, '60s, and '70s. The biggest names in jazz for me at the time were still Miles Davis, John Coltrane, Charlie Parker, Dizzy Gillespie, Art Blakey, and Monk. All the guys from the bebop and smooth jazz era in NYC. But the California jazz radio stations played West Coast jazz people like Gerald Wilson, Wes Montgomery, Shorty Rogers, Frank Morgan, Chico Hamilton, and Dave Brubeck. For me, this was the golden age of jazz; besides, it was the only jazz music I had. I also had quite a few R&B records by Stevie Wonder, Michael Jackson, The Stylistics, Al Green, Aretha Franklin, James Brown, and Motown.

In San Diego, I saw about three or four concerts at the Catamaran featuring Carmen McRae and Nancy Wilson. I also saw Pharaoh Sanders at UCSD. He played a couple of pieces that I really enjoyed, such as "The Creator Has a Master Plan" and "Upper & Lower Egypt." Pharaoh had sleigh bells, tambourines, triangles, and a number of drums in his percussion section. They played these instruments at the beginning and end of all his songs. He used the piano, guitar, bass, sax, and trumpet as solo instruments. This was a very unusual concert, but good.

My career was about to change again in a big way. I took a job with Sperry UNIVAC, a computer company that developed hardware and software for mainframes or large computers. In this job, I worked on mini-computers and microprocessors as a systems programmer using assembly languages. This job was at Point Mugu Naval Air Station in Oxnard, which is about eighty miles north of Santa Monica. Oxnard was a small farming town in Ventura County. You are not going to hear a lot of live jazz there. I was told that this was a temporary assignment, and it would last about six months, but it lasted almost two years. Since I believed that Point Mugu was a short-term assignment, I left my family in Solana Beach during the week and spent the weekends with them. After nine months of this arrangement, the whole family moved from Solano Beach to Newbury Park, close to where I worked.

During my temporary residence in Oxnard, I shared accommodations with Ralph Smith, who was both my colleague and a fellow programmer. Ralph grew up in Hawaii, where his father was stationed with the Navy. Ralph attended Navy-based high schools and the University of Hawaii, where he studied computer science. He had been following jazz and R&B for several years and introduced me to Miriam Makeba, Hugh Masekela, Jonathan Butler, and Al Jarreau. All these musicians, except for Al Jarreau, were from South Africa. They were living in the United States in exile. Their music was a mixture of jazz, protest, and South African tribal music. Some of their music sounded like American folk songs with African rhythms and influence.

When I first heard this music, South Africa was going through apartheid, whereby Black South Africans were made to live separately and subserviently to Whites in every way. They did not have South African citizenship or civil rights. All of these musicians were refugees as they could not go back to their country for political reasons. If they went back, they would be imprisoned. The Black South African musicians wanted the world to know about their imprisoned leader, Nelson Mandela, and their living conditions back home. They protested through their music, political rallies, and the news media.

I did not know this at the time, but I would later have some connections with these musicians again, especially Al Jarreau. I saw him in jazz concerts on television and in Europe multiple times between 1980 and 2010. I met him once in a hotel in The Hague, where we were staying for the North Sea Jazz Festival. He was performing, and I was a fan. He was very friendly and talkative. We met at breakfast. I was in the breakfast buffet line trying to decide what to eat. All the food was foreign to me, so I was taking my time. I heard people behind me getting impatient, so I told them to go around me. When I looked up, the people behind me were Al Jarreau and his band. Al then started singing, "It is great to have choices. Take your time." I replied, "Al Jarreau, I saw you in concert last night." He laughed and asked me if I liked the concert. I said yes, then he asked me if I wanted to join them for breakfast. I politely declined and told him that I was sitting with some other people.

I never met Miriam Makeba, but when we lived in Scottsdale, Arizona, in the early 1980s, we had a Black student from South

Africa stay with us. After a few days in the United States, she became very homesick. Suddenly, the United States became alien to her. She missed her friends and culture, namely her language, music, dress, and food. We could not do anything about her friends and food, but we had some Miriam Makeba and Hugh Masekela records. After hearing Miriam Makeba sing "The Click Song" and Hugh Masekela play "Grazing in the Grass," she cheered up and started to cry. She was so happy to hear songs in her native tongue sung by her national heroes. She loved the records so much that my wife, Carole, gave them to her. Later, I saw Mariam Makeba and Hugh Masekela in concert at the North Sea Jazz Festival in The Hague. They had great concerts. The crowd loved the music so much that they gave them a standing ovation.

We lived in Newbury Park for a year, then I took a job assignment in Seattle. I was still working for Sperry UNIVAC as a contractor for the Boeing Aircraft Company. The work site was Everett, WA. My specific job was to consult and meet with Boeing's customers as their representative software engineer, and to identify and analyze problems in microcomputers, such as M6800 and Z80, embedded in the Boeing 767 and 757 aircraft. These airplanes were the first commercial airplanes to have digital computers. In addition, our job was to design, implement, and test software on the new Boeing aircraft.

We lived on Mercer Island, and I commuted about fifteen miles to Everett every day. Seattle was a dry period for me in the jazz department. I did not go to any jazz concerts. However, I listened to my jazz albums on my stereo and radio. The only concerts that I saw were R&B groups Earth, Wind, & Fire and The Commodores.

After two years, we moved to Scottsdale, AZ, where we saw Lou Rawls at the Hilton Hotel, and Luther Vandross at a Phoenix downtown auditorium. The Lou Rawls Concert was held outside in the grass in ninety-degree temperatures. We sat on lawn chairs. The performance was wonderful. Lou Rawls and his band were excellent, but it was hard to enjoy it because it was so hot. Luther Van Ross played downtown Phoenix at the Civic Center. His concert was sold out. He performed on a rotating stage with many flashing and colored lights. Some women tried to run on stage to touch or hug Luther during the show. He was cool and did not let that bother him. He just smiled and kept singing.

In Arizona, big-time jazz bands such as Count Basie, Billy Eckstine, and Duke Ellington were frequent visitors. These bands came with great singers like Frank Sinatra, Sarah Vaughan, Lena Horne, and Sammy Davis Jr. I did not go to any of these concerts; however, I managed to see them on television.

- 13 -

GOING TO EUROPE

I LEFT SCOTTSDALE AND THE UNITED STATES to take a job as a contractor for the US Army in Europe in 1985. I worked for the Unisys Corporation, a computer software development company, as an applications programmer. My company had a contract with the US Army at the European Headquarters (USAREUR) in Heidelberg, Germany. The Army organization that I supported was the Forty-Third Signal Battalion of the 178th Signal Company. My job site was at the Heidelberg Communication Center on Campbell Barracks.

I traveled to Heidelberg with my wife, Carole, and son, Robbie. My daughter, Hilary, was in college at the University of California (UC), Berkeley. She came to Europe later in the summer. We arrived in June when high school was still in session. Robbie had just completed his high school sophomore year in Arizona, but Carole thought it would be a great idea if Robbie could enroll in Heidelberg High School to make new friends, although there were only three weeks left of school in the year. Heidelberg High School was a school for Army and contractor dependents. The high school was in Campbell Barracks. Everyone there was a US military ID card holder. The school was under the direction and regulations of the Department of Defense Dependents (DODD).

Living in Heidelberg as an Army contractor was a new experience for us. We had to follow Army and NATO laws, regulations, and rules. We were required to have military ID cards, driver's licenses, and ration cards. We had the privilege to use the Post Exchange (PX) and Commissary to buy retail goods and groceries. This Army community had its own bank, hospital, post office, auto dealers and garage, restaurants, hotels, night clubs, travel agency, movie theaters, etc., established for military ID card holders. This life was vastly different from living in Europe as an American tourist or an expatriate.

When we got to Europe, we lived in a German hotel named The Queen's. It was about five miles from the base. We stayed there for three months until we found an apartment in August of 1985. We moved into a complex on Konstanzer Strasse Four. This apartment building was six stories high and had about 200 apartments. Its occupants were half American families and half German families. The Americans who lived there were active-duty military, US government employees, and contractors. These apartments were on the German economy and had nothing to do with the Army.

We made friends with several active-duty soldiers and their

families. Carole's best friend was Elizabeth "Lib" Maynard. She was from North Carolina and married to Sergeant Clarence Maynard. They had two children, a girl and a boy. Other new friends in the apartment were the Thomas and Newkirk families. Renee and Sergeant Humphrey Thomas became our family overseas. Carole called them her children and adopted Renee as her second daughter. The Thomases had two children when we met them. Later, while in Germany, they had two more girls. We went to all of their family's birthday parties and spent several holidays with them.

The Newkirk family lived upstairs. Their son, Charles "Bucky" Newkirk, went to high school with our son. They were the same age and in the same grade. The Newkirk family had great house parties. They invited us to most of them, where we met several other American neighbors: Brenda and Bernard, Roberto and Edna Cruz Pagan, and Bobby Rolette. During our years in Europe, all these friends were frequent visitors to our apartment. We went to many of their parties and social events.

One of my pastimes in Heidelberg was playing pickup basketball with the local neighborhood boys at the apartment playground. These kids were primarily German and Turkish high school and university students who lived in the apartment complex. They were between sixteen to twenty-two years old. My favorite basketball players were Johan, Stephon, Dörsen, and Matthius. While playing ball, we talked about their lives, dreams, and what it was like living in America. These guys knew all the great American professional basketball players like Michael Jordan, Magic Johnson, and Larry Bird.

Robbie had many friends in Heidelberg. Some of them were German, like Markus and Mausi Lott, a.k.a. Christina. They were siblings who lived downtown above their family's fabric store. They came to our house to visit Robbie every day during his last two years of high school. Robbie had many American friends as well. They were his high school buddies, Walter Wilcox, Tony Ortiz, Ty Young, and others who accompanied him to school and sporting events, concerts, clubs, and streetcar trips downtown. Robbie played soccer for Heidelberg High School and the local German youth team. He was selected to the All-Europe Soccer Team for DODD high schools in his senior year. He also received three scholarships for soccer to attend American universities. Robbie was also the first American to play in the German Youth League for the Baden-Württemberg Region and was voted the outstanding player in that league. His high school and German Youth League coach was Claus Prezant. Robbie was also a member of the high school ski team.

In the late summer of 1985, Hilary arrived in Germany. She immediately got a job as a clerk within the Community and Family Support Division at Campbell Barracks. The next summer, she interned at the US Army Hospital across the street from the apartment. She became friends with a female soldier whom she worked with from West Virginia, named Tina Blaney. Hilary left UC Berkeley and started school at the University of Maryland in Munich at the US Army Base McGraw. After she graduated from there with an AA degree, Hilary worked for the Army Finance Department in Heidelberg for a year. She made several friends there, too.

Over the next several years, Hilary learned German and had German friends like Katie Weber, Sandra Rowe, Britt Krambs, and Eva Diehl. She went all over Germany with these girls. They were her road buddies. They visited many of the American military bases and danced at the enlisted clubs, such as in Mannheim, Schwetzingen, Stuttgart, Darmstadt, Kaiserslautern, Frankfurt, Karlsruhe, and more. In other words, they partied all over Germany.

When we purchased anything off the base in the German economy, we had to use German currency, the Deutsch Mark. Today, the German currency is the Euro. Every day, the dollar rate to the Mark or Euro changes. You had to be aware of this rate when exchanging US dollars to Marks or Euros. Marks and Euros were typically obtained at the Bank of America on base. We got a better rate there.

After getting established in the military community, we ventured out to downtown Heidelberg and its surrounding areas. Hauptstrasse is the main street in downtown Heidelberg. It is a pedestrian walkway about two miles long. Retail stores, bakeries, coffee shops, restaurants, and fast-food stores line this street. We went downtown Heidelberg on the weekends to walk around, shop, and have coffee and pastries. We also walked to Heidelberg Castle whenever we could. This was one of the biggest tourist attractions in town.

The Christmas season is a special time in Germany. We went down Hauptstrasse to the Christkindlmarkt, or Christmas market, every year. We would stay there for three or four hours wandering around shopping. The first thing you notice about this place is the smell of roasted chestnuts, wurst, and glüh-wein. In this market, they sold food, beer, candy, Christmas trees and decorations, clothes, shoes, and small children's toys. The Christkindlmarkts were extremely popular and crowded. They start the first week of December and go on until Christmas Day.

On some weekends and holidays, we traveled all over Western Europe. We went to France, Luxembourg, the Netherlands, Belgium, Switzerland, Italy, Spain, the Czech Republic, Austria, Denmark, and England. These trips usually cost between $100 and $150 due to my military discounts and benefits. This was a cheap way to see Europe. These trips were bus tours with many Americans accompanying you. Some of the more memorable trips were to Berchtesgaden, Rome, Copenhagen, and Spain. Some of these trips were sponsored by the Army's Morale Welfare and Recreation (MWR) program.

One of the best trips was a weeklong ski trip to Berchtesgaden, Germany, in the middle of the Bavarian Alps. This place is famous. It was created by Adolf Hitler during World War II as his getaway resort. They call it Hitler's nest or hideaway. This trip was sponsored by MWR and the Forty-Third Signal Battalion. It included free ski clothes and lessons in English, room and board in Army hotels, and transportation. This was an exciting trip because my family and I were going to learn to ski at a mountain resort in the winter. The first thing we had to learn was how to put on ski clothes, boots, and skis. Next, we had to stand up and maneuver over small hills using ski poles. This all may sound easy if you've done it before, but you must be coordinated, motivated, and physically fit. My children caught on to skiing right away. In three days, they were skiing on the intermediate and advanced courses. My wife and I took more time to master the basics. In addition to skiing, we took time to discover the area, shop, and taste regional cuisine. We also took a nice horse and buggy ride to King Ludwig's Castle and visited several Bavarian villages.

Another great trip was the visit to Rome, Italy. This trip was taken during the Easter holidays and was a five-day historical tour. We had a professional Roman tour guide who gave us the history of the Colosseum, Vatican, St. Peter's Square, Trevi Fountain, and the Spanish Steps. He also gave us lectures on the Roman Emperor Constantine and how he became the first Roman Pope, as well as Jesus's disciples Peter and Paul, and how they got to Rome. This was an amazing lecture on the city of Rome, Christianity, Constantine's conquest of Jerusalem, and the Roman Empire. My family and I then visited the Vatican Museums and the Sistine Chapel, which house many ancient religious artifacts, statues, and paintings. The most famous paintings were by Michelangelo and Raphael. Since this was the Easter holidays, we were fortunate to witness Pope John Paul II give the Easter sermon at Saint Peter's Square.

We visited Spain's Costa Brava region on another weeklong MWR-sponsored trip. We stayed in Costa Del Mar and Barcelona. The highlights of the Spanish trip were the beaches along the Mediterranean, ancient Spanish architecture and buildings, and the food. The works of famous artists Pablo Picasso and Salvador Dalí are displayed all over the Catalonia region.

I joined Kappa Alpha Psi, a Black college fraternity, in 1988. This chapter of the fraternity is called the Germany Alumni

Chapter. I was surprised that it had about a hundred members stationed all over Europe, affiliated with the Army and Air Force. Most of the members were military officers who graduated from Historically Black Colleges and Universities. The requirements for joining the fraternity were having a four-year college degree from an American college, being invited to join by a Kappa member, having a US military ID card, paying the fraternity dues, and being willing to go through the fraternity initiation and ceremony, a.k.a. pledging. Once you met these requirements, you were part of the Kappa Alpha Psi Fraternity.

My sponsor to join the fraternity was Dr. George Palmer. He was a heart surgeon at a German hospital. He was also a Kappa Alpha Psi life member and ID card holder. Dr. Palmer was a native Jamaican. He attended Dillard University in New Orleans as an undergraduate, then received his Doctor of Medicine from Heidelberg University's School of Medicine in Germany.

My best friend in the fraternity was Eddie MacArthur, a.k.a. Mac. He was a retired Army Sergeant Major who was married to Sergeant Major Susie Stephens MacArthur. When we lived in Germany, and after I joined Kappa Alpha Phi, I talked to Mac two or three times a week. We went to all the fraternity functions together and exercised together by walking four or five miles around the town where he lived. We remained friends after we returned to the US

Being a member of Kappa Alpha Psi had many benefits, especially in Europe. We had yearly events such as a Black and White Ball, a New Year's Eve Dance, and the famous Kappa Disco Train Ride in June. Between 100 to 200 people attended the

Kappa events. The most popular event was the Kappa Disco Train Ride, with about 500 to 800 people. The fraternity rented a German passenger train for the weekend. The train started in Heidelberg and went to Koblenz, a town in the middle of German wine country. This train ride goes along the scenic route up the Rhine River. The train arrived in Koblenz around 9 p.m. Then you would debark and go to a three-story dance hall and begin to dine, listen to music, or dance. We partied in this building for four hours. Then we got back on the train and partied all the way back to Heidelberg until about 8 a.m. the next morning.

The Kappa Black and White Ball is a formal event that is put on by all chapters worldwide. All the ladies wore white formal evening gowns, and the men wore black tuxedos. In Germany, the Black and White Ball was held in a sixteenth-century palace that was the residence of the last prince of the Heidelberg area. This event is free for Kappa members and their dates as well as for invited Kappa supporters who paid for past events.

All the fraternity events were fundraisers except the Black and White Ball. The money that we raised as profits from fraternity events contributed to scholarships for high school student dependents stationed in Europe who had held a B average or above and did not have the economic means to go to college.

While in Europe, the fraternity was a major social outlet and a way of maintaining an American life overseas. When I pledged to become a Kappa, my line brothers were Don Hamilton, Lee Harvey, Pete Gray, Don Brown, and Alp. They were all Army officers, except Lee Harvey. He was an Air Force Major, and he was elected to be our fraternity line president. The dean of pledges was John James, a.k.a. JJ. He was an Army Captain and a helicopter pilot. It was his job to make sure that all of us pledges passed all the tests and examinations, and demonstrated worthiness.

Europe was a place where we continued our education. During the twelve years that we were in Germany, Robbie graduated from high school and started college at the University of Maryland's (UM) global campus. In addition to an AA degree, Hilary got a BA in business from UM and a BA in international economics from the American University of Paris in France. Carole received a BS in social work from the UM overseas and started her internship at the Army Hospital. I took graduate courses in information systems from Bowie State University overseas. I fulfilled all the course requirements for a master's in information systems except the practicum and research. All these courses that we took were taught at night at Heidelberg High School.

We had two tours of duty in Germany. All the incidents and adventures mentioned in the above paragraphs happened on the first tour of duty from 1985 to 1990. In 1990, we went back to the US for nine months, because my Army contract in Heidelberg had terminated. We were transferred back to Phoenix, in a section of town named Paradise Valley. I worked as a subcontractor for Honeywell Corporation as a systems analyst. This branch of Honeywell designed, implemented, and tested software for aerospace companies like Boeing, Lockheed, Airbus, Northrop Grumman, etc.

Carole got a job working for Maricopa County as a contract social worker for the Child Protective Services Agency. This was a tough job. Her clients were children, mostly teenagers, who were living in bad family situations or who had committed crimes. Some of these children were murderers, rapists, thieves, and bullies. The courts removed them from their homes for neglect, abuse, or because their parents could not control them. Many of these kids did not attend regular school. Some of them were locked up in children's detention centers. Carole's job was to visit these children and their families and to develop a working plan or program that would help them have a better and more normal life. Once she developed a plan, it had to be approved by the County Department of Child Protective Services and a county Judge. She then had to represent these children in court, and her clients had to abide by the ruling of the court.

Robbie enrolled in a local junior college and started taking courses. Hilary applied for Arizona State University's Law School and was accepted.

After nine months in Phoenix, my job terminated, and I was transferred back to Heidelberg, Germany.

– 14 –

Montreux Jazz Festival

WE STARTED GOING TO CONCERTS in Europe in 1986. I found out about the Montreux Jazz Festival (MJF) by accident. One week in June 1986, the company clerk, a guy named Tony, said the Army Company that I was assigned was going to the MJF in Switzerland for a week. This trip was sponsored by MWR for active-duty military members and their families in Europe. Initially, I thought the MJF was just for soldiers, but the company clerk said that my family and I could go if there was room on the bus, but we would have to pay for our hotel rooms and concert tickets.

Fortunately, there was room on the bus! So, my wife, son, and I were on our way to the famous MJF. This was our first jazz festival in Europe. Quite a few people in the company went on the trip, including jazz enthusiasts Norm Wilbon, Ivan Bonilla, and Bobby from Detroit, along with about a dozen other people.

This made for a potentially good and exciting trip because I knew everyone, and they were all nice people.

We stayed in a family-owned pension hotel in Territet, Switzerland, a small town just outside Montreux. This was an old three-story hotel where everyone on the same floor shared a bathroom. It was a little inconvenient, but it was clean, cozy, and neat.

In the 1980s, the jazz festival's concerts were held at the Montreux Casino. You could gamble on the first floor, at the ground level, and upon entry. The concerts were performed in concert halls on the second and third levels underground. Today, the MJF is held at a huge glass and steel building named Stravinsky Hall and various outdoor places along the lake. Montreux is a resort town on Lake Geneva. This section of Switzerland's primary language is French. Montreux is conveniently located on the opposite end of Lake Geneva, a.k.a. Lake Leman, with the city of Geneva at the other end. Many Europeans and Swiss vacation in Montreux every year. Surrounding the town are the French Alps on one side and Swiss vineyards on the other. There are lots of boats and swans in the lake. Montreux is very scenic, especially during the summer when flowers are in bloom and the smell of palm and citrus trees permeates the air.

The MJF lasts two weeks. It is not only a jazz festival, but a carnival and county fair all in one. As a result, hundreds of Swiss and Europeans attend this festival every day but never go to a concert. They walk up and down the lakeside promenade buying food, clothes, and souvenirs instead. There are about 200 tents where vendors line both sides of the walkway and sell their goods and wares. Some of the tourists and residents listen to free concerts outside, or ride merry-go-rounds and other circus rides. This is a yearly festive family event for the locals.

Musically, the MJF in 1986 was a particularly good year. The headliners were Miles Davis, David Sanborn, Wynton Marsalis, George Duke, George Benson, Chaka Khan, Anita Baker, just to name a few. We stayed at the MJF for a week. We walked around the lake to the concerts every day. The concerts that I liked best were George Duke, David Sanborn, and Anita Baker. During the David Sanborn concert, a member of his band, bass player Marcus Miller, walked through the audience playing. He then played a solo in a seat next to my wife! Carole took a fan and started fanning him while he played because he was sweating. He and all the people around us were amused.

This was Anita Baker's first trip to Europe and the festival. A soldier named Bobby from the company said he went to high school with Anita Baker in Detroit. Somehow, he managed to fight through the crowd and get to her. He came back with Anita and introduced us to her. She gave my son, Rob, a big hug. The other person we met was George Duke. He had this giant gold medallion around his neck. My son asked him for it. George replied, "Are you crazy? This thing cost me a pretty penny. You think I am going to give it to you." Rob was disappointed. We also met Wynton Marsalis.

Over the years, we saw some very memorable concerts at Montreux including Prince, Herbie Hancock, Mavis Staples, Carlos Santana, Kool & The Gang, Lionel Richie, Earth, Wind & Fire, and a special concert for Quincy Jones's seventy-fifth birthday featuring Patti Austin, Patrice Rustin, Joe Sample, James Ingram, and others.

In the '90s, MJF changed its venue from the casino to Stravinsky Hall on the main street of Montreux. The main concert hall is upstairs, and the small concert hall is in the basement. The smaller concert hall is called the Miles Davis Club, and it is arranged like a big city nightclub where tables and chairs are set up around the stage. When we went out to eat during the festival, we met all kinds of people and American fans from all over the United States. One time, at a table in a restaurant sitting next to me, I met a couple from Atlanta who said they were the managers of Leuteres.

I also had some strange things happen to me at the MJF. I experienced one of the most unique concerts in Europe. I saw an English R&B band, The James Hunter Six, which played American music from the '50s and '60s. They performed music by James Brown, Five Stairsteps, Frankie Lymon, and old street corner group-type music. They had a great concert; the crowd was singing along and dancing to every song. At breakfast, my daughter saw James Hunter and members of his band sitting at a table in the back. I did something that I normally don't do. I walked up to their table. However, it was not him. When I told this group of European men that I enjoyed their concert last night, they looked at me like I was weird. No one said a thing. When I went back to our table, my daughter told me that I had gone to the wrong table. I was so embarrassed. I did not go to any more tables, but later that day, I got a chance to redeem myself. We saw James working on one of the hotel computers in the lobby. This time, my daughter identified him, so I said, "Excuse me for the interruption, but I really enjoyed your concert last night." He was very pleasant and courteous. He said that he patterned his music after American R&B artists of the '50s and '60s. He also talked about his musical background in the UK and how he was raised listening to Black music.

In 2019, we saw Jamaican guitar player Ernest Ranglin perform with his group at the festival. He is one of the lesser-known jazz artists, but quite an accomplished musician. Ernest was in his seventies when we saw him. The important thing about Ernest's group was their music. It was outstanding. They played Caribbean and African music with a strong drum and guitar beat. They also had Courtney Pine on saxophone. I thought Ernest Ranglin was the best musician that we saw that year. And there's more, he and his wife stayed at the same hotel as we did, the Royal Plaza. We saw them at breakfast. Unfortunately, he did not look well, and his wife was very protective of him as he was suffering from Alzheimer's disease. She kept everyone away from him.

We then did not go back to MJF until 2022, because of the COVID-19 pandemic. This year, we skipped all the paid concerts because they featured rock and roll, folk, and local musicians. The artists were not well-known, and their music did not have complimentary reviews. So, instead, we walked up and down the promenade along the lake, sightseeing and visiting the Lake House Library, where I met I met the director. We discussed the library's uniqueness, how it housed the album covers and sample music of all the musicians who had performed at the MJF.

That is a novel idea and a great educational tool, but it does not go quite far enough. I suggested to the director that if he changed a few things, the library could become a world-class attraction and a jazz museum.

I think the Lake House Library should include a brief history of jazz, music from the all-time best-selling jazz recordings, jazz standards, as well as sample listening of several types of jazz, like bebop, swing, ragtime, etc. The library could also explain, demonstrate, and exhibit other music genres that influenced jazz, such as the blues, R&B, gospel, and European classical music. I believe that people from all over the world would visit the Montreux Lake House year-round if these changes were made. Unfortunately, the director never replied to my email.

After MJF that year, we drove to Interlaken and Grindelwald, Switzerland. Interlaken is a town between two lakes, Brienzersee and Thunersee. It is also the best way to drive to the top of the Alps. The village that is at the top of the Alps is Grindelwald. It resides between three mountain peaks, the Monch, Jungfrau, and Eiger. This area is very picturesque and a main tourist attraction. We stopped there and had lunch. Later, we spent the night in Interlaken, then drove back to Montreux.

In 2023, we stayed at the Eden Au Lac Hotel with a lake view room. The main artist of this trip was Maluma. He was the number one Latino artist in South America that year. His music is very energetic and upbeat. The audience knew all his songs and sang along with him. I liked his concert, but I did not like the concert arrangement and accommodations. We had to stand for two hours in a crowd of about 500 without air conditioning.

– 15 –

North Sea Jazz Festival

IN 1987, THE SUMMER after the first MJF, the guys in the company informed me that the largest jazz festival in Europe was the North Sea Jazz Festival (NSJF). This event was held the second weekend of July every year in The Hague, Netherlands until 2006. Today, NSJF is held in Rotterdam.

NSJF is a three-day jazz festival with fifteen concerts performed simultaneously in one facility. The concerts are conducted primarily in one building with a few acts held outside in tents and in an amphitheater. The feature artists are American jazz musicians. Since there are so many concerts at one time, it presents many scheduling conflicts. This means you must know the lineup in advance to make intelligent concert choices. However, the good thing about NSJF is that if you do not like a concert, you can go to another one in a different music hall.

When we first started going to NSJF, we stayed at a beach town just outside of The Hague, named Scheveningen. It is a resort town with a casino and nightlife. People from all over Europe go there for vacation. In those days, we stayed at the Ibis Hotel and ventured up and down the boardwalk all day until it was time to go to the concerts. Besides watching people, the boardwalk is a beautiful place for food. You can buy hamburgers, pancakes, pizzas, ice cream, or any other kind of food. Every morning, we ate breakfast, hit the beach for a few hours, then went back to the hotel to rest for the concerts. After a short nap and shower, we took a streetcar to The Hague. This was our NSJF routine.

The NSFJ shows that we saw in 1987 were: Count Basie Orchestra, Monty Alexander, Miles Davis, The Crusaders, The Robert Cray Band, B.B. King, Dexter Gordon, Cab Calloway, The Manhattan Transfer, Rockin' Dopsie, Taj Mahal, Wynton Marsalis, Albert Collins, Stanley Jordan, George Benson, Dizzy Gillespie, Kenny G, Randy Brecker, Chuck Berry, and Ornette Coleman.

The next year, in 1988, we saw: Miles Davis, Kenny G, Lionel Hampton, David Sanborn, John Lee Hooker, Red Holloway, Jack McDuff, Shirley Horn, James Brown, Yellowjackets, Eddie Palmieri, Carlos Santana, Horace Silver, Eartha Kitt, Art Blakey, and Ray Charles.

I am forever grateful to NSJF for giving me a chance to see the great Latino musicians such as Tito Puente, Eddie Palmieri, Carlos Santana, Ray Barreto, Joe Cuba, Dave Martinez, and Chucho Valdéz. I really enjoy their music. Afro-Cuban jazz and salsa music from Spanish Harlem with the Latin percussion section, horns, and piano makes me want to dance every time that I hear it.

My sister, Wilma, accompanied me to NSJF in 2005. It was another unusual year. We began in Amsterdam doing the tourist things like visiting the famous sites, restaurants, and museums. Then we proceeded to The Hague, where the NSJF was held in those days. And then the excitement started. As we were boarding the train in Amsterdam, I got on with my luggage and my sister's luggage. Then the train left the station, leaving my sister standing on the platform screaming! I went into a panic because I had my sister's passport and train tickets. We were incredibly lucky because a station official saw the entire incident. He called the train and told them to tell me to get off at the next stop and wait for my sister. When Wilma arrived, she was angry and told me to give her the passport and tickets now. She also said, if you ever leave me again, she was going to have her boys beat me up. It took her a couple of hours to calm down.

Around 2006, NSJF moved from The Hague to Rotterdam and into a new facility. This place is very modern-looking, with round glass and a steel structure. It's called the Ahoy Arena, and it is a larger complex than the one at The Hague. Most concerts are held under one roof, and the acoustics are better than The Hague. However, all the hotels are in central Rotterdam, which is a long way from the Ahoy, where the concerts are held. They moved NSJF from The Hague because it is where the congress and legislative branch of the Netherlands reside. Congress, there, needs to conduct political activities year-round, and NSJF prevented them from having summer sessions.

Rotterdam is a port city at the intersection of the Rhine River and the North Sea. Therefore, it is a convenient transportation and shipping hub. It's also Europe's largest seaport. In Rotterdam, we stayed at the Inntel Hotel. It is located on one of the harbor inlets in the center of the city. This hotel is on a street near the subway and about four subway stops from Ahoy. We know some of the people at the Inntel Hotel on a first-name basis now, particularly the kitchen staff. Our favorites are Rudy and Isaac.

The year 2015 was another wonderful year at NSJF. This was the year that we were the special guests of Lionel Richie at the courtesy of Curtis Battle, Lionel Richie's road manager at the time. He is a friend and former teammate of our cousin. Being a special guest meant that we had backstage passes and could eat at the musicians' dining room for free. We saw the Lionel Richie concert backstage about twenty feet away.

The COVID-19 pandemic made us miss a couple of years of NSJF. We were back in 2022. I was not going to miss NSJF again, "come hell or high water," because we paid for concert tickets, partial airfare, and the hotel a couple of years in advance. If we did not go, we would lose a lot of money. That year we saw: George Benson, Lizz Wright, Marcus King, Diana Ross, Gregory Porter, Trombone Shorty, Christone "Kingfish" Ingram, Eric Gales, Erykah Badu, Nile Rodgers & Chic, Cory Wong, Dave Koz, H.E.R, Charles Lloyd, Bill Frisell, and Alicia Keys. The first night, George Benson had a great concert and a good group of musicians. He performed his hits: "On Broadway" and "Give Me the Night." Lizz Wright did folk songs and some gospel tunes. She performed with the Rotterdam Orchestra. It was okay, but very mundane and subdued. The surprise of the night was Marcus King. He looks like a country singer but was listed as a blues singer. He is a country, rock and roll, and blues singer, and he combines all these styles into his music. Marcus has a good voice and great delivery. The last two acts of the night were Diana Ross and Gregory Porter. Both were great shows. They performed their hits. However, the main thing that I remembered about the Diana Ross concert was the extreme heat. It was hard to enjoy the music because we had to fan ourselves to stay cool. She did the same while performing on stage, as the NSJF did not have air conditioning.

Trombone Shorty started the next night off with a bang. He and his New Orleans jazz band were very energetic and upbeat. They came on stage playing "When the Saints Go Marching In" and kept it going until the end of the show. His band consists of seven musicians and three singers. This concert was especially satisfying for me because we met his saxophone player, B.K. Jackson, a couple of weeks earlier at the Hampton Legacy Jazz Festival in Virginia. Catfish Ingram and Eric Gales were the following acts. They are blues bands from Mississippi and Louisiana who play down-home and Muddy Waters-type blues. The last show of the night was Nile Rodgers & Chic. They were outstanding. Nile Rodgers named some of the songs that he wrote for other R&B and pop stars like Madonna, David Bowie, Sister Sledge, and then did segments of each. He ended the concert with "We Are Family" and "Get Lucky." He encouraged the audience to sing along.

The final night began with Cory Wong featuring Dave Koz. This was an incredibly good modern jazz quintet. Cory Wong played guitar, and Dave Koz played the saxophone. Next, we saw Charles Lloyd featuring Bill Frisell. This was the best old-school jazz performance at NSJF that year. They played jazz standards from the '60s, '70s, and '80s, including "Flower Jazz Song" and "Round Midnight." Although Charles Lloyd was old, he was still good. The last two acts were R&B artists H.E.R. and Alicia Keys. They played their hits, and both had good and entertaining shows.

In 2023, NSJF launched with two great performances by Van Morrison and Buddy Guy. Van Morrison is in his eighties but still has a strong voice. His band consists of drums, guitar, piano, washboard, harmonica, saxophone, bass, and vocals. They played gospel with "This Little Light of Mine," folk songs like "It Takes A Worried Man," country western, and many blues songs. All the background music was country. Buddy Guy played some of Muddy Waters hits like "She's Nineteen Years Old," "Got My Mojo Working," "Hoochie Coochie Man," and "Mannish Boy." He is still a blues legend. Buddy also did a medley of guitar players who he liked such as B.B. King, John Lee Hooker, and Jimi Hendrix, and played their songs in their guitar styles.

Wynton Marsalis and the Lincoln Center Orchestra were entertaining and professional. Wynton is a mature and older man now. He sat at the back of the band, where he directed every song and motion. He occasionally played trumpet solos. You could see how he mentored and tutored them. They played several jazz standards. Another big band that we saw was Charles

Tolliver with the New Rotterdam Jazz Orchestra. They played a few Coltrane, Ellington, and Monk tunes. The saxophone, piano, and bass players were outstanding. Charles Tolliver did not play but directed the orchestra. We also saw Marcus Miller and Kenny Garrett, who gave their usual great performances. They played multiple instruments and had audience participation while doing the hits.

The last night at the NSJF in 2023 was the best. We saw Samara Joy, Seal, Gregory Porter, and Lizzo. Samara Joy is in her twenties and has already won three Grammy awards. She sings in the styles of Sarah Vaughan, Ella Fitzgerald, Carmen McRae, and Nancy Wilson. But the star of the night was Lizzo. She is very energetic and charismatic. She sang and danced for two hours. She also championed fat girl and LGBTQ causes with her songs. Lizzo invited a ten-year-old girl from the audience to come on stage and join her. The little girl played the drums with the band for a short session. It was awesome.

– 16 –

Jazz à Juan

THE THIRD JAZZ FESTIVAL that we attended in Europe was Jazz à Juan. It is held at Juan-les-Pins, France, in the suburbs of Antibes. Jazz à Juan occurs every year in the second and third weeks of July. These concerts are held outdoors in a theater of chairs on the sand and bleachers facing the Mediterranean Sea. Watching concerts there is very scenic; when looking at the stage, you can see boats and yachts passing by. But there is only one stage; all the other jazz festivals in Europe have multiple stages and concert halls.

Some of the same famous American jazz musicians who play at NSJF and MJF also play at Jazz à Juan. The only difference about this jazz festival is that some of the performers are French, African, and Middle Eastern, and they all play their versions of jazz. It's quite a variety of music. Another difference, this jazz festival concludes with the last day being free and devoted entirely to gospel music. We saw some great acts there, including Keith Jarrett, Sonny Rollins, Lucky Thompson, Al Jarreau, Gregory Porter, Marcus Miller, Lionel Richie, Stevie Wonder, Kenny Garrett, Branford Marsalis, Wayne Shorter, Tom Jones, and more.

Juan-les-Pins is a part of the French Riviera. It is conveniently located between Nice and Cannes. From Juan-les-Pins, you can take a thirty-minute train ride to Nice or a sixty-minute train trip to Monte Carlo, Monaco. Usually, we stay at the AC Hotel Ambassador Antibes-Juan-les-Pins. Sometimes in the morning, I took leisurely walks along the beach from Juan-les-Pins to Cannes. It is about a two-mile walk. Juan-les-Pins has a famous pedestrian walkway where outdoor restaurants line the street. While eating at these restaurants, you can see celebrities from all over the world, such as movie stars, professional athletes, musicians, and European royalty. The featured foods on the menus at these places are grilled chicken, beef, lamb, and pork, as well as fresh grilled vegetables. Pasta, pizza, and Greek salads are also extremely popular. I've tried them all.

This area is also known for its museums and art. In Antibes, we visited the Picasso Museum and, in Nice, we visited the Modern Art Museum. There we saw artworks by Henri Matisse, Pierre-Auguste Renoir, Vincent van Gogh, Marc Chagall, Claude Monet, and others. We also visited Monte Carlo. There we saw Jacques Cousteau's Oceanographic Museum of Monaco, the casino, and the palace.

We have our favorite places to eat in Juan-les-Pins.

Sometimes, in the mornings after a leisurely walk along the beach, I stop by a place called the Corner Restaurant for coffee and pastries. One day, I met an American couple there who overheard me talking to the waiter. They immediately asked me if I was a musician playing at the jazz festival. I told them no, that I was just a fan. They then told me that they were kind of famous because the husband of the couple was the lawyer for Barry Gordy of Motown Records. These people had heavy Brooklyn accents and a lot of expensive gold and diamond jewelry. They looked like rich American tourists.

Just like the other jazz festivals in Europe, special things happened to us here, too. We got premium seats close to the stage of a Lionel Richie concert thanks to his road manager. A few rows over, we saw Magic Johnson and his family and friends. Lionel Richie invited them to come on stage and join him with his last song.

In 2018, we saw Tom Jones in concert. We sat behind two men. One guy was from England, and the other one was an Irish fisher currently living in Juan-les-Pins, France. They were best friends and attended this concert because Tom Jones was from Wales and a friend of the Englishman's family. They stood up and sang all the songs. After the concert, they went with us to have a pizza and accompanied us back to the hotel.

Jazz à Juan in 2022 was a good year. Again, this was the first year back after a two-year absence because of the COVID-19 pandemic. The first concert played "Cross Currents," featuring Dave Holland, Chris Potter, and Zakir Hussain. The main event of the night was Gilberto Gil. He is a guitar player from Brazil, and he plays music native to his country. He had about twenty family members in his band. They spanned three generations, and they all played instruments, sang, and danced. Gilberto Gil and his family stayed at the same hotel that we stayed at. We saw them the next morning at breakfast. Gilberto was behind me in the buffet line. He said, "Good morning, how are you doing?" in perfect English without an accent. I was surprised because he was polite, nice, and he knew that I was an American. I told him that I was doing fine and that I enjoyed the show last night. He thanked me, then continued to breakfast with his family.

The next night, we saw the Joey Alexander Trio and Diana Krall. Joey Alexander is a piano player. He and his group are young and classically trained musicians. They played a modern and smooth brand of jazz composed by them. Diana Krall is also a jazz piano player and singer from Canada and is in her fifties. She performed jazz songs by Nat King Cole, Frank Sinatra, and the old jazz legends. However, everything she did was soft, slow, and uninspiring.

The last night at Jazz à Juan featured the Tigran Hamasyan Trio and the Herbie Hancock Quintet. Tigran's group was an average modern jazz group. Tigran Hamasyan is a pianist from India who spent some time studying American jazz. Herbie Hancock had Terence Blanchard as his special musical guest. Blanchard played trumpet and composed a couple of tunes that the band played. Herbie played some of his hits like "Maiden Voyage" and "Rockit." The crowd loved his music. Herbie had a great concert.

One strange thing about jazz festivals in Europe is that most people think Black Americans are musicians. Since Herbie Hancock and his band stayed at the same hotel we did, some of the hotel staff and guests called *me* Herbie. I had to correct them and tell them that I was not him, but just another American fan and tourist.

In 2023, the highlights of the festival were Lizz Wright, Brad Mehldau, and Branford Marsalis. Lizz Wright's band was excellent, especially the guitar and organ players. They played jazz, blues, and gospel in great fashion. Lizz Wright stayed in the same hotel as we did. She had a lengthy conversation with my daughter about jazz concerts in Europe and Black American participation.

That year, we met interesting people who were not musicians.

The taxi driver who drove us from the hotel to the Nice airport was from Venice, CA. He was indigenous and went to the same high school and community college in Santa Monica as my wife. He moved to France because his wife was French, and she wanted to live in Europe. We talked about the hot spots in Santa Monica all the way to the airport. We also met an interesting couple from Malaysia who were stockbrokers. The husband was about ten years older than his wife, and he had recently retired. They have been going to the Jazz à Juan Festival for some time. This year, they sat beside us for the Branford Marsalis concert. The couple told us that they rent a condo for a month every year and go to concerts in Nice and Juan-les-Pins. They knew about the Marsalis family and had followed their music. In fact, the couple had traveled all over Europe and the United States listening to jazz and other genres of music. They knew many of the jazz standards and the original musicians who recorded them. In the last twenty years, they have met many famous musicians. They were very inspiring.

– 17 –

BACK IN THE US AGAIN

WE MOVED BACK TO THE UNITED STATES from Germany in 1996. I was transferred to the Unisys Corporation office in Virginia Beach, Virginia. The boss at this site was Dick Harper. I reported to him for the project in Germany, too. He was a division manager. He was also previously a Marine Corps major and helicopter pilot.

My job here was marketing and systems analysis. The primary task was working on proposals and bringing in new business. I was led to believe if I landed a new contract then I would be made its project manager. However, they assigned the new contract I proposed to someone else. At this point, I asked for a transfer to another office in the Washington, DC area.

We stayed at Virginia Beach for about a year. It was a wonderful location to live because it had beaches, cheap housing, universities, and plenty of places to shop. This place was also great for Carole, health-wise. She enrolled in a physical therapy program sponsored by a local hospital and made many friends. Carole made progress walking and enjoyed the environment.

It was also a good place for jazz. We went to a couple of jazz concerts at Norfolk State University. The concert that I thought was outstanding was performed by Regina Carter. She played jazz on the violin. Her music is a mixture of classical, R&B, and jazz. I could hear her Detroit-Motown background in some of the pieces. Virginia Beach has a free outdoor jazz festival on the beach every summer. They also have a free R&B-funk festival on the last weekend in August. The surrounding areas like Hampton, VA, and Norfolk, VA, have world-renowned annual jazz festivals.

One day in 1997, we moved to Northern Virginia. First, we moved to an apartment in Springfield, VA, then to a new house in Woodbridge, Virginia. I started a new job with Unisys at the Newington office as a project manager in the systems development department. My boss was another former Army helicopter pilot, a Black man named Jim Brayboy. He was a decorated Vietnam War hero. He served in Heidelberg, Germany, as an Army Finance Department head in the 1980s before I was there. I was in this job for about a year and a half until my twentieth anniversary with the company. Then I was eligible for early retirement from Unisys, so I took the opportunity. Unisys's early retirement meant extra income in addition to Social Security later in life. But this retirement income would not start until I was seventy years old.

However, I did not quit working. I started to look for another job immediately instead. I took a job at CSC (Computer Sciences Corporation) as a project manager in Falls Church. Unfortunately, I was not satisfied with this job, so I quit. At this point, I wanted to go back to designing software systems. After working for several small computer companies for two years, I landed a job at the MITRE Corporation as a principal information systems engineer. I worked for MITRE from 1999 to 2019. The office that I worked in was originally located in Reston but moved to McLean, VA, in 2003. MITRE is a not-for-profit company whose customers are the federal government. The organizations that I worked for while at MITRE were the Department of Defense and the Intelligence Community. During the twenty years that I worked for MITRE, I analyzed, designed, implemented, and tested software systems.

Musically, working in this job and living at this location was great for me. I was glad to be in the Washington, DC area. There is a lot of jazz there. Carole and I ventured out to nightclubs and concert halls to see live performances. We went to famous jazz spots like Blues Alley Club and The Birchmere. We also saw wonderful concerts and musicals at Constitution Hall, the Kennedy Center, and the Warner Theatre. Some of these events were classical music, operas, and plays. For example, we saw "A Christmas Carol" and "Carmen."

Carole's health started to decline in 1997. Her multiple sclerosis (MS) came back vigorously. In 1999, she had to walk with a walker. About a year later, she could not walk at all. Then Carole was wheelchair bound. She was in this state for about three years. All her activities were extremely limited.

But she continued to go to concerts, social and business events, doctor appointments, and shopping. However, she had to be accompanied everywhere.

In 2005, Carole was bedridden. She lost the use of her legs and had to be helped with basic mobility and bodily functions. This condition caused her to have an MS attack and internal medical problems. One day, she fell unconscious. When this happened, I called 911, and the first responders took Carole to the hospital in an ambulance. She never got better. At this point, her kidneys were failing, as well as other organs. She stayed in the local hospital in Woodbridge, VA, for a month. Carole's kidneys and pancreas eventually recovered, but she developed bed sores and intestinal problems. Her doctors recommended that she go to a long-term care facility because she was severely disabled with MS and had medical problems. This was not what I wanted. I wanted her home with me so we could be together and share our married life.

After many discussions with doctors and medical professionals, I was convinced that it was best for her and me that she live in a nursing home. We found one in Reston. Somehow, I always hoped that her condition was temporary, and through some miracle, she was going to get better and come home. Carole went to several nursing homes in Virginia and Washington, DC, until we found Manor Care, which was better than the rest.

It really bothered me that I could not take care of her, and that we were both now alone. From 2005 to 2015, I spoke daily with her on the telephone, and I visited with her for at least two or three hours a day on the weekends and holidays. During this time, we talked about the old days when we dated, all the wonderful places we lived, and the people we met along the way. This was our routine until 2015, when she got cancer and died a few months later. We honored her final wishes by having her funeral in a Catholic church in Woodbridge. About fifty friends and family members were at her funeral.

Since then, I've continued our jazz festival tradition. But, I made a promise to Carole that I would always have a travel partner once I reached seventy years old for safety and companionship. Now my travel partner is my daughter, Hilary.

I've attended several in the United States, and I still attend the jazz festivals in Europe as well. Over the years, I attended Capital Jazz Fest in Columbia, Maryland, the DC Jazz Festival, and the Hampton Jazz & Music Festival in Virginia. I saw Joshua Redman, Cassandra Wilson, Stephanie Mills, Frankie Beverly and Maze, Kenny G, Boney James, Gregory Porter, Najee, Charlie Wilson, Gerald Albright, Richard Elliot, Rick Braun, Brian Culbertson, and more.

The Hampton area has two jazz festivals every year, the Jazz Legacy Foundation Festival at the Hampton Convention Center, and the Hampton Jazz Festival at the Hampton Coliseum. In June 2022, we attended the Jazz Legacy Foundation Festival, which was the first year since the pandemic. The performers were Marcus Miller, CeeLo Green, Marcus Anderson, Hiroshima, Regina Bell, Gregory Porter, Marion Meadows, Alex Bugnon, Paul Taylor, Richard Elliot, Kirk Whalum, Keiko Matsui, and Marcus Johnson.

In the spring of 2023, we saw the New Edition Music Tour.

This tour included all the New Edition members from the past, including Ralph Tresvant, Bobby Brown, Ricky Bell, Michael Bivins, Ronnie DeVoe, and Johnny Gill. The other entertainers on this tour were Tank, Guy, and Keith Sweat.

We also attended the Hampton Jazz Festival that year. This three-day festival was an all-star event. It kicked off with Jonathan Butler, Trombone Shorty, Stephanie Mills, and Anthony Hamilton. The next night, we heard the Chuck Brown Band, Chris Botti, Avery*Sunshine, and Charlie Wilson. On the final day, we saw Peter White, Kenny G, Kenneth "Babyface" Edmonds, and Fantasia.

In addition to jazz festivals, we saw many concerts in the DC area at the Kennedy Center, Constitution Hall, and Wolf Trap. These places host all kinds of music and events, not only jazz. Classical music is played there more than any other kind of music. Although one of the best jazz venues in DC is the Kennedy Center, we saw several plays and award shows there as well. In early fall 2023, we went to the Kennedy Center to see the jazz awards show. That year's recipients were Kenny Garrett, Regina Carter, Charlie Mingus, and Louis Hayes. All of these musicians are from Detroit except for Mingus. And each of these artists played a couple of songs, except Mingus, who passed away a few years ago. His wife received his award.

In November 2023, we went back to the Jazz Legacy Festival in Hampton. The lineup was as follows: Damien Escobar, Bob Baldwin and Ragan Whiteside, The Fellas, Boney James, Jeffrey Osborne, Lindsey Webster, Brian Simpson, Sheila E., Will Downing, Jonathan Butler, Steve Cole, Christian Big New York de Mesones, Richard Elliot, Maysa, Howard Hewett and Micheal Lington, and Peter White.

My friend Marcus Gray is the person I've talked to about jazz since we moved back to the United States. We talk at least once a month and discuss new jazz music and concerts. He lives in Montgomery, AL, with his wife Caroline. I met him in Germany when he worked with my wife at the US Army tax relief office. Marcus listens to the radio and constantly shops for jazz music. He has many of the old jazz standards and avant-garde CDs. If he hears something that he likes and thinks is good, he tells me about it and vice versa. He sends me a lot of good music.

I retired from the MITRE Corporation in March 2019, and I retired for good. Now, I finally have time to listen to my music as long as I want, go to more concerts, learn new computer languages, read history books, and write about my life and experiences.

During retirement, I discovered another source of good music—the public broadcasting system (PBS). PBS television has jazz specials once or twice a month and is a great learning tool. I saw programs about Miles Davis, Sam Cooke, Louis Armstrong, Michael Jackson, and many others. Dr. Louis Gates had two great specials on the Black Church and Black gospel music.

- 18 -

WASHINGTON PUBLIC RADIO

I NOW SPEND MANY SUNDAYS listening to the Washington public radio station, WPFW. This radio station's slogan is "Jazz and Justice." Its programming specializes in jazz, blues, and public information concerning social justice, politics, and education. WPFW tries to provide a service that commercial radio does not. This station is funded by listener donations as it has no commercial sponsors.

When I am home, the radio is my background music, information, and noise. The radio is on while I am doing chores, cooking, eating, working on the computer, and watching sports. During the week, I listen to R&B on commercial television and radio.

WPFW is special on Sundays because I can hear the radio shows of Tom Cole and Donnie McKethan. Tom Cole plays a soft and smooth brand of jazz. His show is named "G Strings," and it is primarily guitar music from around the world. Tom Cole is on the radio from 9 a.m. to 11 a.m. In the afternoon, I listen to Donnie McKethan's program, "The American Song Book," from 2 p.m. to 4 p.m. This show features artists like Frank Sinatra, Nat King Cole, Johnny Mathis, Tony Bennett, Sarah Vaughan, Ella Fitzgerald, and others. The main and last segments of his show focus on Frank Sinatra. Unfortunately, Donnie died in 2023. He was replaced by Willard Jenkins, who plays classical jazz music from the '50s, '60s, and '70s, as well as new jazz music performed by new artists.

One of the best radio jazz series was done by WPFW and the Kennedy Center. On Duke Ellington's birthday, the station and the Center dedicated several days to his music and life. The initial program began by saying Duke is the district's favorite son and has had immeasurable influence on jazz worldwide as a pianist, composer, and band leader.

Of course, you cannot mention the most important jazz musicians of Washington, DC, without talking about Ellington. He was born and raised here. The district has named a high school, a bridge, a plaza, restaurants, and sandwiches after him. His name is everywhere. Duke Ellington High School is a music, dance, and art conservatory. To be accepted, you must be a DC resident. In addition, you must have good grades and audition for a position.

The jazz station explained that Ellington gained prominence as an orchestra leader and composer who began at the Cotton Club in Harlem in the 1920s. For the next forty years, Duke had many recordings and performances around the world. Some of his most notable songs were "Mood Indigo," "Satin Doll," and "Take the 'A' Train." He is one of the greatest jazz personalities ever, and I regret not seeing him perform live. The Kennedy Center also had a jazz director named Jason Moran. He and Cyrus Chesnutt performed two concerts commemorating Ellington's birthday. These concerts were from compositions that he wrote later in life. These were some of his lesser-known works that were composed for the civil rights movement and gospel.

One of my favorite WPFW personalities is a man who narrates the blues program on Thursday nights. His name is Scooter Magruder. He was the DJ at my eightieth birthday party. He set up his electronic DJ equipment along with his DJ friend Slow Roll in my living room. We cleared up space in the family room so we could all gather in one place and dance. This event was special because my family and friends were there, including my daughter, sisters, granddaughters, and friends. These people came from all over the country to celebrate my big birthday. They decorated the interior and exterior of the house with birthday balloons, cards, paper, and artifacts. The highlights of the evening were everyone singing "Happy Birthday," eating the cake, and dancing. One of Scooter's big surprises was letting me name my favorite song, and then all the women in the house had to line up and dance with the birthday boy.

We attended a blues festival in Charles County, Maryland, during a birthday weekend. The emcee of the blues festival was DJ Scooter McGruder of WPFW. The same man who played music at my birthday party a year earlier. The featured artists were Clarence "The Blues Man" Turner and Lee Bennett. WPFW was a sponsor of the festival. During the blues festival, Scooter

McGruder asked me to stand up in front of everybody and be recognized as the birthday boy. I was shocked and embarrassed, but I stood up. I felt like a celebrity.

We had another night of jazz in Silver Springs, MD, in May 2024. This concert was held in a nightclub. We saw a trio consisting of a bass, piano, and drums. This group was named the District Collective, and consist of local DC musicians. This event was also sponsored by WPFW as a reward for its members.

My family and I were continually active, listening to live jazz during the Christmas season in 2024. The Saturday before Christmas, Hilary and I went to two parties. The first one was given by the former mayor of the city of Alexandria, VA. This woman is a person whom we met at a "Voices of Motown" concert at the Birchmere, a local club in Alexandria. The event she hosted took place in an elegant bar overlooking the Potomac Riverbank in the city. They played soft and smooth jazz as background music while people stood and ate finger food. She invited politicians, musicians, educators, friends, and family. About one hundred people attended.

The second place that we went that night was the WPFW Christmas Party in DC. This was a dinner and disco dance party. The site of the event was WPFW's radio station. The DJs of WPFW played R&B music all night. After dinner, I danced for half an hour. This was a good night.

I am ending this book with a pledge to you. I pledge that I will see more jazz, blues, and R&B concerts and festivals in the US and Europe in the years to come.

9 781969 679377